The Listening Heart

Best wishes!
Leigh

The Listening Heart

The Limbic Path Beyond Office Therapy

Leigh Shambo, MSW, LMHC

With David Young and Catherine Madera

*A Manual for
The HEAL Model™ of Equine-Facilitated
Psychotherapy and Learning*

HUMAN-EQUINE
ALLIANCES FOR LEARNING

Human-Equine Alliances for Learning (HEAL)
PO Box 84
Chehalis, WA 98532
http://www.humanequinealliance.org/

Printed in the United States of America

© 2013 by Human-Equine Alliances for Learning (HEAL)

Cover and interior design and layout by Karen Bacon

ISBN-10: 1482085089
ISBN-13: 978-1482085082

Except as permitted under US Copyright Law, no part of this book may be reprinted, reproduced, transmitted, or utilized in any form by any electronic, mechanical, or other means now known or hereafter invented including photocopying, microfilm, and recordings, or in any information storage or retrieval system, without written permission from the publishers.

Trademark Notice: Product or corporate names may be trademarks or registered trademarks, and are used only for identification purposes and explanation without intent to infringe.

Because of the dynamic nature of the Internet, any web addresses or links contained in this book may have changed since publication and may no longer be valid.

All photographs and diagrams used with permission. Portions of Chapter Two, all of Appendix A, and some vignettes were previously published in another form, and are used here with the permission of *Scientific and Educational Journal of Therapeutic Riding*.

*For my mother Margaret,
in loving memory and with
tremendous gratitude.*

✝

Contents

ILLUSTRATIONS List of Figures and Photos   viii
PREFACE Leigh's Story and the Birth of HEAL   ix
ACKNOWLEDGMENTS   xv

INTRODUCTION Meeting the Challenges of EFPL in Clinical Practice   1

Chapter One The HEAL Model in Perspective   7

Chapter Two A New Science of Relationship   17

Chapter Three The First Key: Body-Based Awareness   29

Chapter Four The Second Key: Boundaries   41

Chapter Five The Third Key: Mending the Divided Self   53

Chapter Six The Fourth Key: Yin and Yang   65

Chapter Seven The Fifth Key: New Pathways (in the Brain!)   77

Chapter Eight The Sixth Key: The Successful Social Brain   91

Chapter Nine Jessica's Story   103

Chapter Ten The Listening Heart   109

AFTERWORD The Remuda   113
APPENDIX A HEAL-Sponsored Research   117
APPENDIX B Practitioner Pathways for EFPL   131
REFERENCES   133
INDEX   137

Figures and Photos

Figure 1. The Tri-brain and ANS   18

Figure 2. Divisions of the Mammalian Nervous System   20

Figure 3. Table of Six Key Affective Domains   24

Figure 4. The 0-10 Point Arousal Scale   34

Figure 5. Nested Hierarchies of Control within the Brain   39

Photos 1 & 2. Boundary Exercises   45

Photo 3. Equine Greeting Ritual   47

Figure 6. Bottom-up and Top-down Processing   75

Photos 4-9. Driving, Drawing, Mirroring   76

Photos 10-11. Clicker Training with Dixsi   85

Figure 7. Panksepp's Integrative Emotional System for Social Affect   93

Slides 1-12. Research Summary Shambo   120-125

Slides 13-23. Research Summary Zasloff   127-130

PREFACE

Leigh's Story and the Birth of HEAL

Students are curious how I came to specialize in this therapeutic modality called equine facilitated (or assisted) psychotherapy and learning (EFPL).* But it was really not like I aimed toward this path; it was more like the path found me, step by step. The journey started with two personal tragedies in one year that changed my life.

I call 1988 the year of my 180. I was 30 years old and my goals at the time were simple: build my skills and reputation as a horse trainer and riding instructor. I was willing to work hard to succeed in an equestrian career. I loved horses and they had been my refuge, a resilience factor for a lonely youth. When I embarked on a career as a horseperson, horses also became a stage on which my abilities, and vulnerabilities, were displayed. And that was not always easy.

In the spring of that turnaround year, I went to evaluate a small sorrel mare as a potential lesson horse for the riding stable I managed in Issaquah, Washington. A lifelong horsewoman, I knew what to look for and what questions to ask. Noting the irregular muscle development in her neck I asked, "Does she have any problems—head tossing, for instance?"

"No, nothing like that." The young woman didn't meet my eyes. When I asked her to ride the mare before I tried her myself, she sat passively on the horse, with no contact from her legs or reins, allowing the horse to wander at will. There was something suspicious about her actions and what came out of her mouth. It didn't add up.

Irritated by the waste of time, my mind rushed to judgment: *She can't even ride.* The longer I watched the more obvious the problem appeared to me. I knew what good horsemanship looked like and she didn't have it. Though my instincts told me the mare wouldn't be a good fit for our program I wanted to make a point. "Let me ride her."

If I knew then what I know now about emotion and behavior as it exists in all mammals, (starting with

---

* Speaking generally, equine *assisted* therapies often denote the horse's role as a tool of the therapist. In *facilitated* therapies the horse is given a larger role to actually lead the process at key points in EFPL.

myself) I'd have never gotten on that mare. But I was a tough cowgirl, confident that I could impose my will on the horse and the situation. It took only moments for a contest of wills to become a wreck—the horseman's term for a dangerous accident. The mare reared high, flinging herself backward and falling on top of me. In a flash I went from confident horse trainer to hospital patient.

BEGINNINGS

I grew up in a suburb outside Chicago, Illinois, the daughter of a "modern" psychologist (client-centered, as opposed to Freudian), and a vibrant "liberated" woman. My mother worked full time as a journalist, was active in civil rights, and was a passionate feminist before the term was even invented. She was a role model to many women, including me, and appeared a stellar example of the mentality of the 1970s—"You *can* have it all." Because my parents were outwardly successful it was easy to ignore the cracks in the veneer of our family: my dad's drinking, the arguments, and disconnection from each other.

As siblings (I was between an older brother and a younger sister) we stuck together and *did* express ourselves. My brother and I imagined we were ranchers in the greenbelts surrounding our home. With make believe horses to carry us to safety, our younger sister was the little girl who needed saving. In another game our sister was the headmistress of "Mo's Home for Children," and my brother and I were abandoned children housed there. My psychologist father did not seem to notice his children were playing 'orphanage.'

Mom's first love was work, not home; and she valued a type of parenting she jokingly (?) called "benign neglect." It was good to foster our independence in this way, she believed. While psychology and philosophy were fodder for dinner discussions in my highly educated home, the rest of the time we largely looked after ourselves. In the era of free love, encounter groups and open marriages, my parents hoped to raise liberated children who knew how to take care of themselves.

There were bright spots, one being that my parents indulged my passion for horses. After paying for three years of lessons, my parents decided it would be cheaper to buy their ten-year-old horse-crazy daughter the ultimate lesson: a Welsh pony named Little Bit. After that, Mom dropped me off each afternoon at the country farm where we boarded him, and I practiced the crude, blissfully ignorant horse handling common to children. Little Bit taught me and took care of me as we navigated countless miles of country lanes and woodlots. Finding comfort in the rhythmic motion of his bare back, I learned that the care one receives from nature, while sometimes harsh, was less confusing than the care I received from my own human family.

I became self-reliant and learned to survive, but I did not learn to value and care for myself. As I came to adolescence, these factors added up to poor self-esteem, an unmet need for loving attention, and a lack of clear values. It was the perfect recipe for sexual victimization—the kind of experiences that I now call 'Little t trauma'—not life threatening, but life degrading. I retreated from people and settled into a series of entry-level jobs working with horses. I married a like-minded man, who guided mountain pack trips.

Along the way, I'd decided psychology was a waste of time. My parents' education had failed to create a secure family, to connect us to each other or to keep me safe from the perils of growing up female. It hadn't fixed my mother's anger, or helped my father support an independent wife who, in later life, spiraled deeper and deeper into depression. That's where she was in 1988, when I turned 31; her life was also a wreck in the making.

Though we didn't share the horsey gene, Mom and I shared many other personality traits. I wanted to be just like her—independent, passionate, physically strong and determined. Maybe that's why I chose a career with horses—manipulating a 1,200 pound animal isn't for wimps. After earning a bachelor's degree in agriculture with a specialization in equine studies, I managed riding stables, taught horsemanship, and guided wilderness rides. I enjoyed retraining problem horses and starting young colts under saddle. Though I put myself in physical danger every day, fear was not a problem. I did not allow myself to feel such a vulnerable emotion.

CRUSHED

As I lay in that hospital bed after my accident, pelvis broken in three places, one thought played over in my mind: *What made me get on that horse?* For the first time in my life I felt whispers of something new and impossible to ignore. I felt fear, but not of the horses. I was afraid of feeling helpless, and of allowing others to help, afraid to have my strong body physically disabled. I was afraid that my willpower would not always protect me; I had to admit it contributed to the wreck.

Mom came to "help me" immediately after my accident. But she was so depressed herself we hardly communicated. She'd already been hospitalized for depression, three times. It was obvious something deep inside was wrong. Here I was, badly injured, and unable to help her or even know what to do or say. One day I simply reached across the kitchen table and took her hands in mine. Her capable hands that had written letters for worthy causes, felt listless in mine. Mom said not a word as I squeezed her hands, each of us lost in a private misery. Just pick yourself up and keep going. That's how we both operated.

Later in that same year, 1988, I received a phone call from my brother, Chris. "Leigh," his voice was steady, but I sensed an emotional undercurrent. "Mom got hit by a train. It's, uh … not really clear that it was an accident." As he talked I had the sensation of living outside my body. Later we found Mom's suicide note and matter-of-fact statement that she wanted us to simply accept her decision to die and move on. At the funeral people spoke about her inspiring life and strong character while I struggled to make sense of it all. *What happened to that proud, independent and self-possessed woman?*

During the months after Mom's funeral I knew I was in trouble. My pelvis healed, but emotionally I struggled. I felt strangely angry and deeply afraid to love others. To make matters worse, for the first time in my life I experienced fear when riding horses. Though I didn't want to think about my pain and the source of it, I was terrified to end up like my mother—or my father who, day by day, disappeared further into the alcoholism that would eventually take his life. In desperation I sought help from a therapist and Al Anon.

THROUGH THE EYES OF A HORSE

Despite my emotional baggage, there were horses to ride and train. High on my list was a young bay mare named Frieda. Athletically talented, Frieda was aloof and independent. She didn't trust or submit easily. Day after day I worked with her, but her defiant behaviors escalated. When she started rearing high to avoid forward movement I stopped riding her altogether and began working her in the round pen using techniques of trainer John Lyons, with the horse at *liberty*.* I memorized the steps used by Lyons, one by one, to get the horse's attention and practiced them on Frieda and the other horses I worked with. Some days I felt success with every horse, other days I felt as stuck as Frieda herself.

The round pen steps were simple, yet despite following them closely there were days the horses resisted. On one such day I contemplated another independent spirit, a BLM mustang called "Stang," brought to me for gentling and starting under saddle. Though Stang would not approach, from across the pen his deep brown eyes were honest and penetrating. A new thought filtered into my brain: *Could he be reacting to me?* Stang lowered his head, and took a tentative step toward me.

After that I noticed a pattern. On the days I was emotionally receptive the horses responded favorably; on the days I was angry and hard they mirrored my internal battle. The horses seemed less interested in the outward techniques I used and more aware of the emotions I tried to hide. They appeared to perceive what was going on deep in my spirit. How could that be possible?

In my personal therapy and through 12-Step work I gradually released and processed a lifetime of painful emotional baggage. The effect on the horses I worked with was astonishing. The horses were like living biofeedback. It was easy to let down my defenses with them, and I was reliably rewarded by a more willing and whole-hearted attitude from the horse. My heart was changing in profound ways. Frieda and I mended our relationship and she responded to the point where she could be ridden safely—eventually with no tack at all. Defenses and fears that had held me prisoner slowly disappeared. Tentatively I allowed myself to feel and connect with humans.

In the year 1988, *something* "turned me around." Suddenly I was looking inward, encountering myself

---

* Liberty training refers to work with no restraining ropes, bridles or harness; the liberty is physical, spatial, and psychological. Cues are emphasized rather than commands.

instead of trying to master outer circumstance. A decade of healing followed, exploring many of the threads of mind-body-spirit connection that are part of the HEAL Model today. The horses that I owned and trained during this period played an important role in my healing and liberation. Although my first marriage did not survive, I began to connect with a wider circle of people using the feeling-based, in-the-moment methods I was learning from the horses.

CONNECTIONS

In 1996, misfortune again created the conditions for personal change, when catastrophic flooding devastated my region (Lewis County, WA). I was hired by a mental health agency (Cascade Mental Health Care in Chehalis, WA) to help screen flood survivors for mental health effects. Later, this agency hired me to implement a psychiatric vocational program for people with severe mental illnesses. The program didn't involve horses, but I implemented relational principles I'd learned in the round pen, such as:

- Small steps successfully completed yield more than big steps that fail.
- Relationship comes before performance; performance follows relationship.
- Actions speak louder than words; *inner qualities of being* guide actions.

The program was a success, and I earned my agency's support in returning to school to earn an MSW, which I finished in 2000. *Personal growth, horses, mental health. I was beginning to see the outline of a much bigger picture.*

Further searching revealed the newly growing professional field of EFPL. I was inspired by the book *Horse Sense and the Human Heart* by Adele and Deborah McCormick (1997), and signed up for a course through Equine Assisted Growth and Learning Association (EAGALA, see references). In December 2000, with co-founder Larissa Fore and early board member Jerre Redecker and others, we birthed Human-Equine Alliances for Learning—HEAL—a non-profit organization supporting equine-facilitated mental health.

Over the next several years I availed myself of several training pathways in EFPL. I attended three EAGALA trainings and two EAGALA conferences, and one workshop with the Drs. McCormick at Hacienda Tres Aguiles in Texas. In 2002, I took a workshop with Linda Kohanov (Epona Equestrian Services) and Kathleen Barry Ingram, a woman destined to become a mentor and friend. An apprenticeship at Epona followed in 2003 and two other programs of advanced study at Epona added to my formal education in equine-facilitated mental health practices and therapies. Kathleen Barry Ingram helped form and launch the HEAL Facilitator Training Program (FTP) and was co-teacher in the FTP from 2008-2010. I'm grateful for Kathleen's contributions to this book and to my professional and personal life.

Because of my background as a riding instructor, I am a longstanding member of Path International (formerly known as NARHA), and have taken the basic therapeutic instructor training workshop. These studies are in addition to the continuing education and supervision hours required of me as a licensed professional; and what I have learned teaching college psychology part time. All of these perspectives have added something to the HEAL Model. It's a pathway for healing and recovery based on the mammal-to-mammal bond with a horse. From this bond, people can develop new templates for human relating and connection. We hope you enjoy reading about it!

ACKNOWLEDGEMENTS

It would be impossible to thank all of the people who have contributed so much to the integration that is now the HEAL Model of Equine Facilitated Psychotherapy and Learning. My thanks would have to start with mentors and teachers who helped me understand the horse, not to mention the horses themselves who often paid the price for my human clumsiness. It would extend to those friends and professionals, and 'inspirationals,' who helped me make the move from surviving to thriving. My gratitude list would have to include my supervisors and colleagues who encouraged my mental health training and education, who instilled in me the conviction that all clients deserve a therapy experience that helps them get well. Like a ripple effect my gratitude extends as well to the colleagues and teachers that share this amazing field where humble horses enable profound healing. To each of the individuals who shone light along the way, I hope you know who you are and feel my heart reaching out to touch yours.

I especially want to thank those who have agreed to share their own experience of healing—the clients who became anonymous research subjects, and Jessica who gracefully and even eagerly decided to share her story. These people feel that the horses helped them recover in a way that no human really could, that the horses somehow helped them to understand and relax around other people. Without this conviction from our most important customers—our clients—this book would not be here today. Thanks to all of my clients who inform and teach me, at least as much as I do them.

I also wish to thank the organizations that helped in organizing and implementing the research: St Peter's Hospital in Olympia, WA and Cascade Mental Health Care in Chehalis, WA. I extend this appreciation to my colleagues in this research as well: Susan Seely, Heather Vonderfecht, and Randy Zasloff. And for allowing the reprinting of selected portions of previously published articles, my hat is tipped to the editors of *The Scientific and Educational Journal of Therapeutic Riding*, official journal for the Federation for Horses in Education and Therapy International (HETI).

At the most practical level, I would like to thank the people whose dedicated work helped bring this book into being. The boundless encouragement and support of my husband and co-author David Young not only made this book possible, but kept it alive when the tasks and projects of daily living threatened to smother it completely. Co-author Catherine Madera contributed her writing, her ideas and her understanding, and her hard work. David and I are grateful too for the friendship that evolved around our project. Designer Karen Bacon agreed to take on editing as well and design duties, and I want to thank Karen not just for her hard work but also for her sincere encouragement and insight as she helped me through one of the most emotionally vulnerable times of the entire process! And the tireless Ricki Martin, HEAL Operations Manager and office guru, who helps with all of the nuts and bolts of documents, communications, and translations! Without these members of the writing and production team *The Listening Heart* would not have found you, the reader, today. Enjoy!

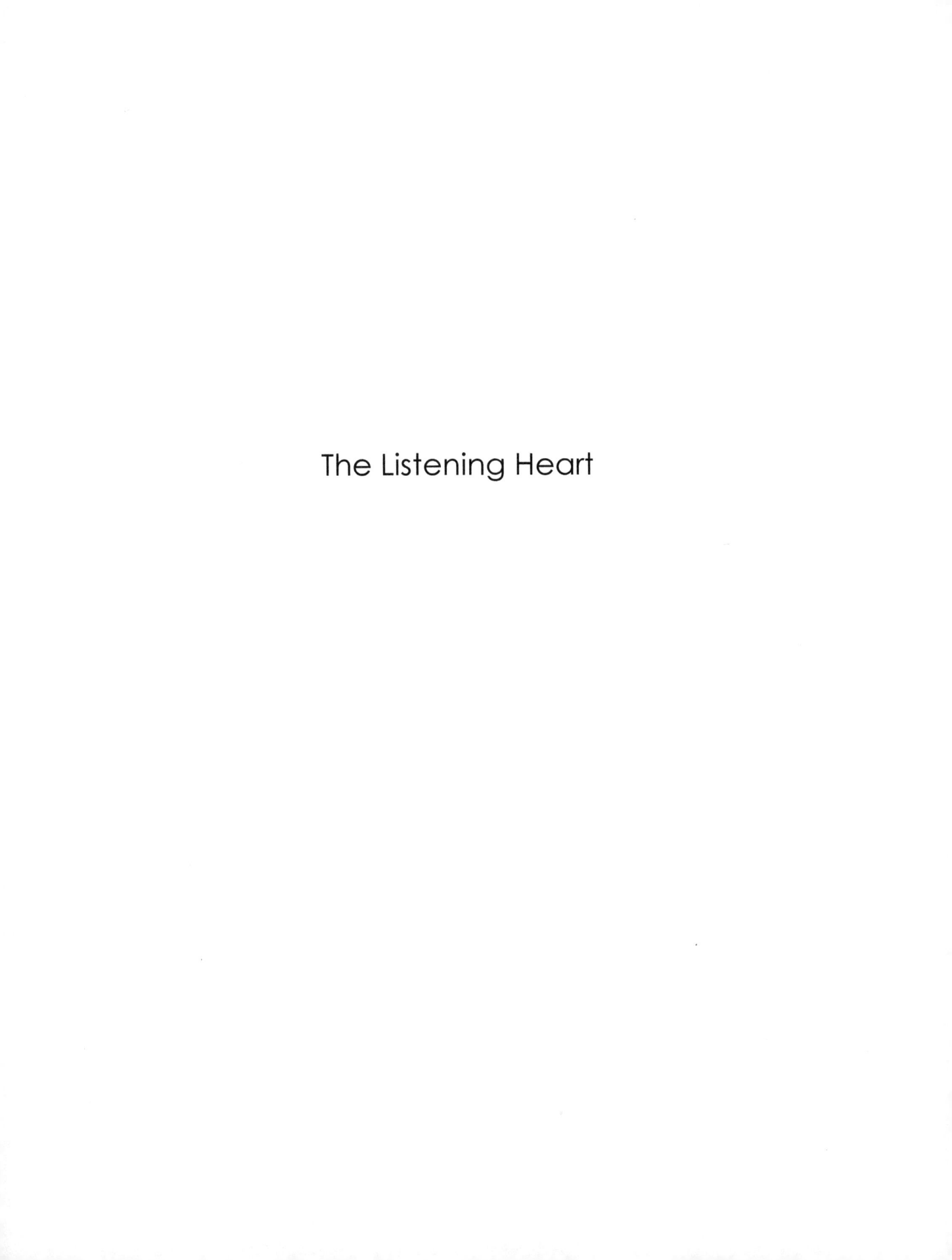

The Listening Heart

INTRODUCTION

Meeting the Challenges of EFPL in Clinical Practice

Incorporating Equine-Facilitated Psychotherapy and Learning (EFPL) into clinical practice is exciting, and also fraught with challenges and responsibilities. The EFPL practitioner must be a qualified therapist, and experienced with client problems and treatment. A thorough familiarity with the horse's body language and behavior is essential to safety and EFPL effectiveness. This dual skill set is often embodied in a practitioner team, which must function smoothly in order for the emotionally sensitive horse to focus on the client(s). The physical site must be safe, humane, and private enough for complete emotional safety. EFPL requires, seemingly, the most complicated treatment setting you can imagine.

Yet, according to Hart, work with horses "… offers a peak experience, perhaps unmatched by any other, with a totally unique physical experience while in a joyous social environment." (Hart, 2000, p. 94) Equine therapy can be highly motivating, and illuminating, for clients who may be difficult to treat in conventional therapy.

It is precisely that ineffable, almost magical quality often found in EFPL practice, which makes it difficult to explain. This is especially true in traditional health and mental health settings where there is an emphasis on "evidence-based practice." Evidence-based practice is a good thing— "… a thoughtful integration of the best available evidence, coupled with clinical expertise, it enables health practitioners of all varieties to address healthcare questions with an evaluative and qualitative approach." (University of Minnesota Libraries, see References.) An important part of our mission at HEAL involves sponsoring and supporting research into the efficacy of EFPL as practiced at HEAL.

GATHERING EVIDENCE

In 2006 I had the chance to test EFPL by a clinical study. "Taking the Reins" was a therapy group/research study, which met weekly for ten weeks. Six wounded women, with chronic symptoms of post-traumatic stress disorder (PTSD) or Borderline Personality Disorder. Six horses. Ten weeks of therapy in a HEAL Equine-Facilitated Psychotherapy and Learning (EFPL) group. Even I wasn't sure what tracking their clinical outcomes would reveal in that 2006 pilot study. The treatment/research team took standardized measures at four different points relative to therapy. The last measure was taken four months after treatment.

The results were surprisingly—almost shockingly—significant and robust (Shambo, Seely & Vonderfecht, 2010). Despite the small group size (which inflated the very real possibility of no trends being found), *all six women responded favorably to the treatment*. Scores were significantly and dramatically lowered for depression and dissociative experiences by using EFPL for ten weeks. At the four month post-treatment check-up all six women had gone from moderate or severe levels of depression to the non depressed range. The women had all changed, largely in the same ways (a summary of results is found in Chapter Ten). Despite my reservations, the study turned out to be statistically *more* significant because of its small size.

That pilot study—along with our continuing research and clinical evidence—adds to documented evidence that EFPL works. When I presented these results at the NARHA National Conference in 2007 (now called PATH International—see references), I met David Young, a retired engineer turned horse trainer, who then became an equine specialist for EFPL. David was also fascinated by the success of EFPL for survivors of complex trauma including those with PTSD. We felt an immediate affinity and a friendship grew around our shared interests. In 2009 David and I married, joining our lives, individual talents and our interest and support for EFPL. As a practitioner team working with clients, we discovered we were fascinated by the same questions: Is there an affinity between horses and trauma survivors? What does 'horse therapy' offer these clients that results in significant documented improvements, even after formal treatment ends? We were moved to explore *what* it is about EFPL that works, and *why*.

David's strengths as a scientist and researcher made the HEAL Model even more potent, allowing us to speak a language that is precise *and* still an accurate language for subjective feeling. You will find this manual full of references and concepts from current research in neuroscience as well as psychology, mind-body science and animal science.

A COSTLY THERAPY?

Hand-in-hand with the need to develop an evidence base, cost is a central challenge to the field of EFPL. Cost of treatment is also a central challenge for social services, the health care industry, for third party payers and for those clients paying out of pocket. Provision of EFPL as part of psychotherapy is an expensive and complicated proposition, increasing the cost of providing therapy, in most cases by at least 50 percent.

EFPL requires a significant investment on the part of the hosting site (whether an equestrian facility or a small private horse yard) to be prepared for providing safe and confidential mental health services. The treatment team is often more than one person (clinician and horse specialist), who may have to travel to the EFPL site from their normal setting—all of which increases the expense of providing this service. Clients and referral agencies have a bigger investment too—not just in the dollars paid for services and programs, but in staff time to assist clients to travel outside of town to the therapy site. Many programs are subsidized by charitable fund-raising in addition to fees for service; and some rely on volunteer helpers or leased horses. Each of these naturally adds more complications and layers of relationship dynamics to the treatment setting.

While it is beyond our scope to explore the factors that shape particular practice settings for EFPL, we will make a case that clinical gain *often does* justify the investment that EFPL takes, especially for difficult-to-treat clients. We will also show how amplified limbic* healing for the client is achieved with much less stress and risk for the therapist.

LET THE READER DECIDE

This book is primarily concerned with the clinical and facilitation aspects of EFPL, and helping therapists understand the core principles of partnering with horses to accomplish emotional healing with humans. It also gives an overview of HEAL-sponsored research. At HEAL, we strongly believe that the future of EFPL lies in validating its effectiveness in clinical settings, and articulating a sound treatment strategy in which the EFPL is tied to specific treatment goals.

Our PTSD research is based on data from clients (youth to geriatric) who participated in an EFPL group, as an adjunct therapy to their main treatment in a community mental health clinic. To understand the scope of our diverse clientele outside of these groups, consider the following: Our clients at HEAL range in age from five to seventy-five, though the majority are adults. Most have a history of relational violence, abuse or dysfunction. Clients most often enter therapy to work on current problems (spouse relational problem) or symptoms (anxiety, depression) that they are experiencing. Younger children may risk developmental delay due to abuse, trauma or attachment disruption. Some of our clients have riding as part of therapy, though the majority do not; for many clients riding is contraindicated due to physical vulnerabilities.

This diversity of clientele has helped us articulate a working model, with principles we can track in any human-horse interaction during a therapy session with any client, principles that are always guiding treatment and can be clearly articulated and justified. For many clients, I (Leigh) am the primary therapist, responsible for an assessment, treatment planning and to serve as an emergency contact when necessary. Other clients are referred by agencies or by their primary therapist for equine-facilitated *learning* experiences that contribute to a therapeutic outcome. Many clients are self-referred, drawn to EFPL while exploring avenues of healing relevant

---

* The limbic system in the mid-brain is involved with emotion, memory and with homeostatic regulatory systems; it is the social-emotional center of the brain.

to their own journey, even if they have to pay from their own pocket. Such is the case with Jessica, whose story appears in the following pages. I am grateful to Jessica for sharing with you, the reader, the important role that horses have played in her recovery.

Without oversimplifying the horse, or over glorifying him, we hope *The Listening Heart* will give the reader a grasp of the method and process by which EFPL unfolds with this model, the 'how-to' of actual EFPL practice. This book is intended as a companion volume to our experiential, hands-on training course, the HEAL Facilitator Training Program for EFPL, thus we are assuming an audience familiar with concepts in psychology, human development and the emerging field of neuroscience, which is transforming the mental health professions. We hope to inspire and educate anyone interested in animal-assisted therapies, particularly with horses.

The Listening Heart describes a model for partnering with horses in order to facilitate psychological and emotional healing with people. The HEAL Model of Equine-Facilitated Psychotherapy and Learning (EFPL) integrates the roots of my life and healing, with my professional training. The model integrates a lifetime of horse experience, with hundreds of different horses in my care, with more than 20 years of experience in mindfulness and mind-body practices. My second career as a Licensed Mental Health Counselor includes adherence to standards of assessment, care and evidence-based practice. Because of my own healing, and through my professional training and experience, I cultivated a special interest in topics related to complex PTSD and its treatment with horses. My life path has been shaped, even fueled, by my passion for horses. I did not know where it would lead, as one may not when in the neural circuit called SEEKING. The Six Keys described in this book can help awaken this 'master emotion' in you and in your clients. *Seek, and you too* will *find.*

"Standing next to a horse may not be a cure, but it is a start," said Don Lavender (2006), an EFPL practitioner in the United Kingdom. My own story bears witness to the fact that the keys to a successful future can be found in the shadow of pain. May these tools help you, and your clients if you are a helping professional, to navigate and strengthen the relationships so critical for a healthy personal life.

It is fitting that we open our exploration of EFPL with Jessica's eloquent, subjective description of a therapeutic activity called 'Horse Dancing' during her workshop at HEAL. It is also a fitting description of a new neural imprint for relationship, which can only be birthed from a new experience within a relationship. Find the rest of Jessica's account in Chapter Nine.

A PRICELESS EXPERIENCE
Horse Dancing at a 3-day personal growth workshop

In Jessica's own words:

"We started out slowly, moving back and forth with each other, and I sent him out trotting, then cantering around me. As he bucked in playful joy, my whole soul came alive. He joined

back up with me and we flowed through the length of the arena, our strides matching in harmony. I ran beside him and my heart sang with a feeling of connection and belonging. Tears of acceptance and freedom welled up from my inner being as I watched Galant embody the joy that I felt inside. I was so amazed at this deep connection that opened up to me when I allowed myself to be free, and I was astonished to discover that the result of being authentic was deep connection, not rejection."

With the exception of Jessica's account, all the client names and session details have been changed in the case illustrations in this manual. It is my intention to represent such illustrations accurately given the highly subjective nature of the content.

Chapter One

The HEAL Model in Perspective

A broad working definition of EFPL is given by PATH International:
EFPL is experiential psychotherapy that includes equines.... [using] respectful equine activities such as handling, grooming, longeing, riding, driving, and vaulting. EFPL is facilitated by a licensed, credentialed mental health professional working with an appropriately credentialed equine professional.... [or] by a mental health professional who is dually credentialed as an equine professional.
(Available at http://www.pathintl.org/resources-education/resources/eaat/193-eaat-definitions)

EVALUATING EFPL PRACTICE MODELS

As the popularity of EFPL has grown, several main treatment models have emerged and many different training programs are being offered. Aspiring practitioners wonder what model or training will be best for them. This depends most importantly on the type of client to be served. The EFPL clinician must understand the needs and treatment goals of the clients. What type of program will be engaging and relevant for this client? How will EFPL challenge each client to achieve treatment goals, while providing sufficient physical and emotional safety? Will the benefit and cost compare favorably with other possible interventions? These are important questions with profound implications for shaping the EFPL practice.

EFPL programs vary widely in the amount of structure provided. It is important to consider the amount of structure and protective support built into the EFPL service provision—how physical safety is defined and addressed varies greatly according to the needs of the client. *The more vulnerable, helpless or volatile the client, the more structure should be provided.* Examples of structure include risk assessments, rules such as safety policies that are followed uniformly, more handlers to assist, and closer accompaniment by a trained professional. Structure also includes staff and volunteer screening and training, and may include assistive technologies such as a specialized mounting ramp or other assistive technology.

Examples of highly structured and supervised services include therapeutic riding for children with disabilities, or a prison-based horse training program for rehabilitation of inmates. Examples of less structured experiences include horse-at-liberty-with-person sessions, or activities with several loose horses and people in the arena at once. These are more typical of the insight-oriented therapeutic approaches and are appropriate for more mature, able-bodied clients. The amount of structure should be safely appropriate to the client being served; EFPL effectiveness depends on a good margin of physical and emotional safety, with carefully managed, strategic challenges.

Another important consideration involves the client's level of psychosocial and neurobiological development. *EFPL must fit the psychosocial stage of the client and be a logical fit with treatment goals*. What is the client's emotional age? How has this been influenced by the client's life experience? An adult client with PTSD may become as helpless as a child in the presence of specific triggers. The client's relationship history will influence the relative proportions of office therapy versus horse therapy, which will vary with different types of patients, as does the relative importance of the horse as an attachment object. The practitioner should be aware that not every client's vulnerabilities are obvious at the outset.

Participants in our PTSD groups at HEAL range in life stage from adolescent to geriatric. These life stage specific groups require flexibility from our facilitation team and our horses! The adolescent groups favor challenge and action-oriented horse activities. Some of the geriatric trauma survivors are physically quite fragile and it is challenging to devise safe exercises in which they can practice being directive and assertive with the horse.

It is helpful to understand the historical perspective of the various organizations supporting and contributing to the field of EFPL. There are no right or wrong approaches; there are *differing* approaches guided by a rationale for a certain client group. These groups also vary in how they view the horse as a partner in healing. *Professional organizations supporting the use of horses in therapy have historical roots in service to specific client types or styles of intervention.*

PATH International, formerly NARHA, has traditionally supported therapeutic riding for the disabled. Today the organization is expanding its umbrella to include EFMH (Equine-Facilitated Mental Health). While PATH International carefully avoids endorsing any particular model of therapy, its emphasis on equestrian safety for potentially vulnerable populations is grounded in its history and development as an organization. The horse is seen as a teacher or caretaker providing a safe holding environment as well as appropriate physical and emotional exercise, in a normalizing, empowering and exhilarating environment.

EAGALA, the Equine Assisted Growth and Learning Association, had its inception in experiential education for incarcerated youth—thus the 'challenge approach' is characteristic of their model. In keeping with appropriate treatment goals for this type of client, the emphasis for the facilitator is on the client's cognitive processing and positive choices. The horse is seen as a tool to reflect back to the person the utility of their choices and attitudes.

Less structured approaches, typified organizationally by the private enterprise Epona Equestrian Services (owned by Linda Kohanov), may include energy awareness, shamanic experiences or an emphasis on transpersonal psychology or spiritual growth. In these approaches the horse is often seen as a sage and sentient guide to a more open consciousness. These approaches are more suitable for psychologically mature clients who already possess healthy ego strength.

This book focuses on Equine-Facilitated *Psychotherapy* rather than the broader field called Equine Facilitated *Learning*. It is written to qualified therapists and educators in fields of human growth and psychological healing who are interested in creating an "in vivo" experience for clinical patients. As a researcher and horse specialist at HEAL, David Young has contributed to this model by locating and citing the most recent scientific understandings of human and animal emotional functioning. He says, "We write this book to therapists who want their clients to connect from a place of wholeness."

A UNIFYING THEORY AND INTEGRATIVE APPROACH

The HEAL approach provides a unifying theory and integrative approach to EFPL. Rather than being methodological, the HEAL Model comprises a set of principles that guide the clinician in processing human-horse interactions within a natural relationship that is developing. The practitioner, trained to recognize developmental and psychological issues of particular individuals, will work within the core affective dimensions most relevant to that client, and view the horse as a flexible, always respected partner in healing.

Trauma is an experience that spans age groups and is almost universal in affecting human lives. By design, the HEAL model is trauma sensitive. The term "trauma" covers a spectrum from "Big T" experiences such as severe neglect, physical or sexual abuse, family violence, and psychological degradation. At the lower end of the spectrum "Little t" trauma marks more lives than it misses. The enduring imprint of a depressed or angry parent, a family broken by a spiteful divorce, marked by alcoholism or suicide—even the perfect family that looks like the epitome of proper upbringing—will all leave psychological scars, patterns of functioning that are rooted in survival and desperation.

Trauma can leave a marked imprint on personality when it occurs during development years; but trauma symptoms just as severe can result in adulthood from war experiences, rape or attack, natural disasters and accidents or unexpected loss. Trauma of any size, when left unresolved, robs humans of their energy and vitality. Big or little, it is what we refer to in this book as a person's unresolved history, patterns of surviving that have outlived their usefulness and prevent us from thriving in the present.

THREE LEVELS OF SOUND CLINICAL PRACTICE IN EFPL

The HEAL Model of EFPL, with its focus on using "Six Keys to Relationship," describes a rubric or protocol for EFPL that integrates three levels. These levels are 1) a sound therapeutic strategy and therapist-client alliance, 2) the experiential EFPL sessions, pertinent to the treatment strategy; and 3) the debriefing of the EFPL in order to potentiate the bridges to daily life and improved functioning in human environments. *For EFPL to have the maximum treatment power there will be a strong coherence in all three levels.* The HEAL philosophy focuses attention to relationship in each level: 1) therapist and client, 2) client and horse (with therapist as a resource) 3) client and others (human-human) relationships. The Six Keys are valid and operative at all three levels of the therapy. This gives us a chance to model, reinforce and clarify the basic relationship principles represented in the Six Keys.

The first level, the therapeutic strategy, refers to an assessment and diagnosis guiding treatment. The therapist is responsible for developing an alliance with the client and articulating goals for treatment. The EFPL has to make sense as a pathway toward those goals. A wide range of treatment goals can be well fulfilled with EFPL as part of the treatment plan.

With most of the individual clients at HEAL, I do the assessment and treatment planning, which are in accordance with state law and professional best practices. EFPL will be one part of a comprehensive plan that often includes other interventions as well. Not uncommonly, clients referred by their primary therapist come to HEAL for the EFPL; the treatment plan in this case is usually brief and psychoeducational in nature. In some instances this requires coordination between the primary therapist and me (which necessitates written permission from the client). In some cases our contract is with an agency or organization, to provide EFPL as part of the planned treatment for their clients. Individual situations dictate the responsibilities of sound clinical practice; the clinician must navigate these in accordance with training and law.

In the second level, the therapist will introduce the client to the horses, and support the client in building a working relationship with one or more horses. The relationship with the horses can contain a wide range of specific activities ranging from simple observation and spending quiet time with horses to robust active play in a round pen, creative games and exploration with the horses, and/or riding. Many clients will benefit from grooming, leading the horse, setting simple boundaries and meeting small challenges with the horse (such as leading past a scary obstacle). We strongly encourage the EFPL practitioners to understand and work the Six

Keys, which are important dimensions of relationship for both humans and horses. Attention and care to these Six Key domains can be modeled, practiced and sometimes explicitly taught within the human-horse interactions. The EFPL places the therapist in a new and different relationship to the client; "opening" the relationship in significant and valuable ways.

Finally there is the level of debriefing, helping to make meaning of an EFPL experience and reinforce it. Clients with (sometimes longstanding) clinical disorders will often need significant help in applying concepts from EFPL to their lives and relationships. Art activities, journaling and other expressive arts can serve to anchor the day's learning. Role playing, modeling and homework that reinforces the concepts will elaborate the new neural pathways and push them to take hold. Debriefing happens during and after EFPL sessions for cognitively capable clients, perhaps even providing material for office-based sessions to discuss and apply the learning from EFPL to activities of human life. The therapist documents sessions and progress, and plans for termination when the client is ready. At HEAL we call it a "home run" when we see a client using healthy new behaviors in the human environment. Common examples include new boundary setting, and use of conscious self-soothing strategies.

The goal of the therapy and the EFPL is restorative limbic practice* or exercise, with the development of healthier, more mature psychosocial skills at all brain levels (brainstem, limbic system and cortex). This restorative practice literally allows the brain to remodel pathways of arousal, emotion and meaning, and it expands the client's window of tolerance for emotion and capacity for healthy relationships. This model is especially well suited to clients with a trauma history because it attends specifically to the issue of emotional regulation and increasing the client's capacity for building healthy attachment bonds. "Home runs"—demonstrable skills and new behaviors expressed in the client's natural environments should and will be the natural result.

THE HUMAN TEAM AND THE HERD

The therapist/educator: The HEAL Model is designed for the qualified therapist, who may be cross-trained as horse specialist or work closely with a horse specialist in all horse sessions. The therapist develops the treatment plan, guided by knowledge of the client. EFPL should make sense as a sound pathway toward treatment goals, and may be integrated with other techniques and interventions in the client's plan. In addition to the legal qualifications to practice, the therapist must carry professional insurance for mental health malpractice liabilities; if the practitioner is dually qualified as a horse specialist and if that practitioner ever practices solo, he or she must also be covered by an equestrian liability policy.

---

* The limbic system in the mid-brain is involved with emotion, memory and with homeostatic regulatory systems; it is the social-emotional center of the brain.

Professional educators may not have the same level of legal requirement and liability. However, they should evidence the education and credentials from professional organizations in their field of practice and provide a sound plan for skill building based on their knowledge of the client.

A discussion of the credentials which qualify the lead therapist/educator on the team providing EFPL services, along with a list of organizations providing training and professional support specific to EFPL, may be found in Appendix B.

The horse specialist: The horse specialist informs the treatment planning and implementation by understanding in depth what activities are possible, knowing which horses fit best with various exercises, and having a keen eye for the horse's body language. The horse specialist is ultimately responsible for safety with the horses and in the environment; the horse specialist carries insurance for equestrian related liability (this may also be accomplished by a farm/facility professional equestrian liability policy). Equestrian liability is different from professional malpractice liability or general business liability; *EFPL requires both for complete coverage of risk.*

The co-workers: It is especially important with a clinical population to have a good staff-client ratio, and for the staff to have adequate skills with people and with horses. Clients with clinically significant symptoms may be prone to the same sort of emotion-driven outburst that horses can experience—it is best not to forget this, though it rarely happens. For individual sessions, a qualified therapist with a good amount of horse experience may conduct the session, and it is always a safe practice to have a skilled horse handler nearby. A therapist and horse specialist may also work as a team during individual sessions. To conduct therapy or personal growth groups, it is best practice to have a team of therapist and horse specialist, along with one or two strong assistants—staff or volunteers who are trained to assist.

The herd: The HEAL Model is a model of equine *facilitated*, versus *assisted*, therapy. The difference in the two terms is subtle, but important. In assisted therapies the horse functions more as a therapeutic tool of the human therapist. During facilitated work the horse is treated as a more equal partner to the human therapist and offers support, helps in direction, offers safe connection with the client, aids in detection of emotional incongruence, and helps gently expose shame, insecurity, performance anxiety, and unresolved history.

Many horses can make good therapy horses, though it is important that horses be evaluated to rule out any aggressive or excessively fearful individuals. I have worked with many breeds and herds around the world and I believe that the capacity to be therapeutic is almost universal. The HEAL herd (at our home site in Chehalis, WA, USA) includes from five to eight individuals. They vary in size, temperament, breed, age and gender. At HEAL, by our training and handling practices, we amplify the innate connectivity of horses by blending three approaches, which are central to our therapeutic approach as well.

Basic foundations of good relational training for therapy horses:

1. We provide *good limbic care*, which includes good boundaries, and fair and strong leadership from the humans. It is important the horses are able to generally trust in human gentleness, clarity and fairness, knowing that their needs will be met.

2. We use *natural horsemanship style approaches* to work within the horse's instincts, overcoming their innate fears of predation and helping them learn to work in partnership with us. This training method is softened by our commitment to hold relationship above performance, and our consistent attention to the handler's—and the horse's—affective state.

3. Using *reward-based clicker training*, we train each horse in a small repertoire of task-related behaviors (such as tricks, or number discrimination). This allows clients to see the horse engage in thinking processes while they solve problems and engage in positively motivated behaviors.

LIMBIC HEALING BUILT ON THE BOND BETWEEN PERSON AND HORSE

Moving a person from trauma to healing requires restructuring of emotional response. This restructuring must come through *experiences* that engage the sensitive limbic region of the brain: the brain's mammalian center. It also requires that clients learn conscious strategies to gain influence over the neural pathways of the limbic brain and Autonomic Nervous System (ANS, which usually operates completely unconsciously).

Such sophisticated emotional work requires a trusting relationship, so the client can sense feelings from their own body and sense their partners feelings too. This is really tough for people with deep-seated distrust of other people! But it becomes possible with the help of our tall, four-legged co-therapists. A practical bond of energy and attention can form between a horse and person, enabling coherent and visceral emotional restructuring, and thus astonishing leaps of healing.

In the EFPL sessions the client is introduced to the horses and supported in building a working relationship with one or more horses. This typically continues over a number of sessions—the actual number of sessions depends on the client's needs, goals and progress. Typically we create the emotional building blocks for limbic connection in the early sessions of therapy, starting with simple activities, which lead to more complex activities later.

> *"Countless times I have seen fear turn to acceptance of self ... a person closed to intimacy turn to a horse when they were unable or unwilling to turn to people. Horses are great teachers of connecting."* (Lavender, 2006, p. 32)

The HEAL EFPL horse activities are built around the natural development of a mutually beneficial, working relationship with the horse. Activities range from observing the horses, to approaching, touching, haltering, grooming; synchronous breathing, learning to soothe a nervous horse; practicing boundaries and yielding through leading and groundwork exercises; active free play in a large round pen, using a join-up model softened with a relationship focus; riding, and interactional games and tricks using reward-based training.

> The goal is for person and horse to: A) create a *limbic bond or connection*; becoming curious about and engaged by each other (resonance), B) *build mutual understanding* and shared communication through challenges (regulation), and C) demonstrate a *smooth partnership* through an attached relationship (limbic revision, for many of our clients). In many cases there is evidence that the bond is mutual and the horse is truly engaged. Horses form strong and lasting friendships much the way people do—through the invisible chemistry of emotional resonance. This *limbic resonance* gives EFPL much of its magic.

In the HEAL Model the horses are recognized as sentient partners with opinions, choices and a sophisticated limbic point of view. They are given as much liberty as possible, recognizing that horse and client are entitled to appropriate structure and direction for safety. We never condone force, but do recognize that assertiveness and awkwardness are part of the developing relationship with a large and very physical (while also highly sensitive) partner.

The EFPL therapist (even within a therapist-horse specialist team) should be skilled at reading horse behavior and establishing limbic connection with the horses to be used in EFPL sessions. This requires in-depth experience with horses, including an ability to understand the emotional life of individuals and the herd as an entity. During EFPL session a tri-fold limbic connection is established: client-horse-therapist.

Developing the unique relationships between human and horse over the course of EFPL treatment (ranging from a few, to many sessions) provides endless fascinating opportunities to study the dynamics and mechanics of shared emotion—vivid proof that our emotions are felt by and matter to others. Even seasoned therapists will be challenged to discern and name the varieties of natural emotional contagion, influences of attachment, safety or defensiveness, and even transpersonal experiences that may occur between a person and a horse. In essence, by examining the relationship with the horse we are able to "see" the *subcortical or pre-conscious levels of process* that occur in this particular relationship, and thus also glimpse those patterns that are below conscious awareness in human relationships for the client.

The role assumed by the horse is sometimes mundane, and sometimes breathtakingly majestic. The sensory imprints are vivid and emotionally evocative. The pace of the therapy overall, and each session, allows exploration of the affective processes between client and horse. There is a saying in horsemanship: "You go faster by going slow." The horses' reactions are often slow (horse time) and there are times when an observer might think nothing is happening between client and horse—but it is, watch closely.

> ### ༄ EFPL Case Vignette ༄
> #### Forgiveness Is An Inside Job
>
> Erin entered therapy at HEAL in hopes of shifting the grip of longstanding dysthymic depression. More acutely, she was burdened with feelings of guilt over her recent divorce. She was at a very low point that made it impossible for her to recognize her own positive qualities. In Erin's initial sessions, she learned simple mindfulness exercises, and she found the contact and exercises with the horses soothing. In Erin's first session our old horse Gem was especially drawn to Erin. When Erin struggled with the breathing exercise, Gem buried her face in Erin's solar plexus until Erin felt soothed and was able to relax into the abdominal breathing. Then Erin discovered that soothing herself helped to settle the horses too, making them more receptive to her.
>
> It was in the fifth session that a tall bay mare named Frieda strode forward to meet Erin, who was immediately struck by the regal horse's aura of self-possession. Erin was surprised at certain similarities she shared with Frieda: both were mothers of almost-grown children, both independent females to whom personal space is important, and today, both had reached out to greet each other with eagerness beyond their characteristic reserve.
>
> Before entering the pen with Frieda, Erin felt a poignant desire to have Frieda give her a sign, a physical action signifying for Erin "forgiveness"—some affirmation of her innate worth in spite of her recent experiences. She entered the pen full of hope for this healing connection.
>
> But Frieda moved away whenever Erin made attempts to approach her. Painful minutes passed. This was not what Erin expected from the horse who had approached her in such a knowing way just a short while earlier. What was Frieda saying?
>
> Finally, I gently suggested that Erin contemplate what it would feel like to forgive herself. It took a moment for Erin to grasp what I meant—and then suddenly Frieda looked toward Erin as if for the first time. Frieda casually walked over to Erin, made a small circle around her, and stood by her side. Erin moved to hug Frieda in gratitude, but the gesture caused Frieda to move away again.
>
> This session continued for a half hour. Whenever Erin wanted Frieda to bestow forgiveness, Frieda would move away again. But each time Erin could hold the thought of forgiving herself, Frieda would again join up close by Erin's side, and she would stay there if Erin could stay calm and grounded. The powerful theme of forgiving herself first was relevant for months in Erin's current relationships, and in facing the circumstances of her early life that had long ago robbed her of emotional well-being.

Chapter Two

The New Science of Relationship and the Brain

"Variants of the same emotional language exist throughout the mammalian family, some ... relatively close and accessible to our interpretive instrument, the limbic brain.... The task of emotion science is to excavate this archaic structure, and as it has done so, it has unearthed the very roots of love."
Thomas Lewis, MD, Fari Amini, MD, and Richard Lannon, MD
A General Theory of Love

How can a connected relationship with the horse help the client heal? The answer lies deep within the mammalian brain, in the brain's limbic system and its body-based partner, the Autonomic Nervous System (ANS). The *limbic system* is a set of related structures found in the mid-brain of humans and other mammals. It is located between the primitive, reflex-driven *brainstem*, and the topmost layer of the brain, the *cortex*. This three-part "triune brain"—first introduced by Paul MacLean in the 1960's, remains a commonly accepted schematic in neuroscience today (Panksepp, 1998). The limbic system is of particular interest to therapists, counselors and educators because it mediates our relational, social-emotional learning (Lewis et al., 2000).

Emotion involves all parts of the triune brain, and emotional states are felt physically throughout the entire body, via the ANS. Emotion is designed to unify and move the body to action. The emotional-social reactivity of the ANS includes near instantaneous reactions (a pounding heart), and hormonally-based enduring "mood states" (as in depression). ANS functions include (and are not limited to) heart rate and respiration, blood pressure and distribution, and muscle tension including facial expression.

The tri-brain, ANS and neural pathways evolved to insure survival by functioning as an implicit RESPONSE/MEMORY/PREDICTION system. But trauma can set this complex and adaptive system on a permanent false alarm. Limbic neural pathways develop early, before verbal and logical capacities; they form templates for attachment and belonging throughout life. Trauma, family dysfunction and violence can imprint the mind-body system with hyper- or hypo-arousal, impairing development and the functioning of the reasoning cortex (Rothschild 2000; Szalavitz et al., 2010). Limbic patterns are especially impacted by interpersonal violence, when humans who should provide safety and belonging are abusers.

According to trauma specialist Bruce Perry (2008) the result of chronic threat

> *... is a brain that exists in a persisting state of fear. These trauma-invoked, repetitive alterations have made the child's stress response oversensitive, overreactive, and dysfunctional because of overutilization of brainstem-driven reactions. These primitive reactions, such as dissociation and hypervigilance, were adaptive while the stressor was present. However the primitive reactions become entrenched over time, and the "lower" parts of the brain house maladaptive, influential and terrifying preconscious memories that function as a general template for a child's feelings thoughts and actions.*

Figure 1. Mind-Body Awareness: What you need to know about your tri-brain and ANS

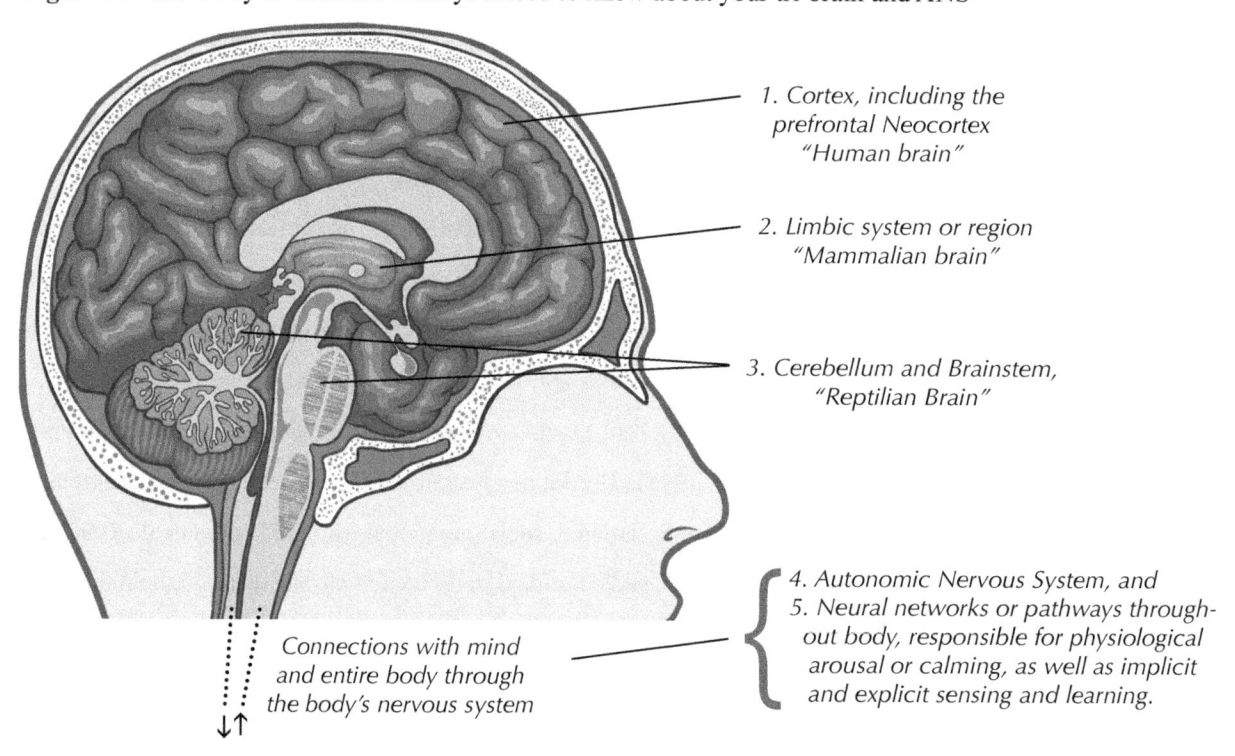

1. Cortex, including the prefrontal Neocortex "Human brain"

2. Limbic system or region "Mammalian brain"

3. Cerebellum and Brainstem, "Reptilian Brain"

Connections with mind and entire body through the body's nervous system

4. Autonomic Nervous System, and
5. Neural networks or pathways throughout body, responsible for physiological arousal or calming, as well as implicit and explicit sensing and learning.

About Figure 1. When didactic education is appropriate for the client, I use the above diagram to educate about five aspects of the mind-body system which will be relevant to our work in Equine-Facilitated Psychotherapy and Learning (EFPL).

1. *Neocortex, or "Human Cognitive Brain"*—is the most recently evolved area of the brain, where we perform high-level thinking, judgment and complex integrative tasks. The frontal lobes are the site of higher level executive functions such as planning and conceptualizing. Other mammals have this part too, but in smaller proportion of the whole brain volume. Called the 'executive region' for its rational capacities, rationality rests on implicit assumptions and non-rational learning from the lower regions of the brain. *This, I tell my clients, is the brain in your head.*

2. *Limbic System, or "Mammalian Brain"*—enables maternal-infant bonding and socialization in mammals. Complex social and emotional behaviors originate in this part of the brain. This is where attachment and bonding patterns are stored. Bonding can become contaminated by threat in cases of neglect or abuse. Limbic reactivity leads to so-called "amygdala hijack"—cortical thinking becomes impossible and reactionary brainstem "fight or flight" takes hold. *This is your emotional brain, intimately connected to your body to your heart (via the vagal nerve), center of the ANS.*

3. *Cerebellum and Brainstem, or "Reptilian Brain"*—regulates basic vital functions such as breathing, heartbeat and motor coordination, as well as the most basic reflexive or instinctive reactions. This is the reactive area that mediates full-blown "fight or flight" (or dissociate and collapse) reactions under conditions of extreme stress. *This is the brain in your gut, the brain of your instincts.*

The three regions of the brain are linked by neurons, somewhat like an incredibly complex road network, connecting the three brain regions through feeling and action states that affect the entire body. For a simple schematic of the Nervous system, see Figure 2. Again—this is primarily for adult clients, an understanding of the following points will be helpful to therapy.

4. *Autonomic Nervous System*—acts as a control and response system throughout the body, coordinating body and brain with environment. The ANS normally functions below conscious awareness to mediate heart rate, respiration, perspiration, diameter of the pupils, and virtually every other aspect of our body-environment adaptation. *This is your personal gauge, which powerfully reflects your feelings. Feelings are a special type of information. One of our purposes is to help you learn about your gauge.*

5. *Neural networks* are the body's primary information system. The brain by itself contains roughly 30 billion neurons, each having some 10,000 contacts with other neurons. It is often said that "cells that fire together wire together." Experience imprints the brain with powerful and enduring habitual patterns of feeling and thinking. *This, I might say to the client, is your history which has locked you into patterns of surviving.*

Figure 2. Divisions of the mammalian nervous system

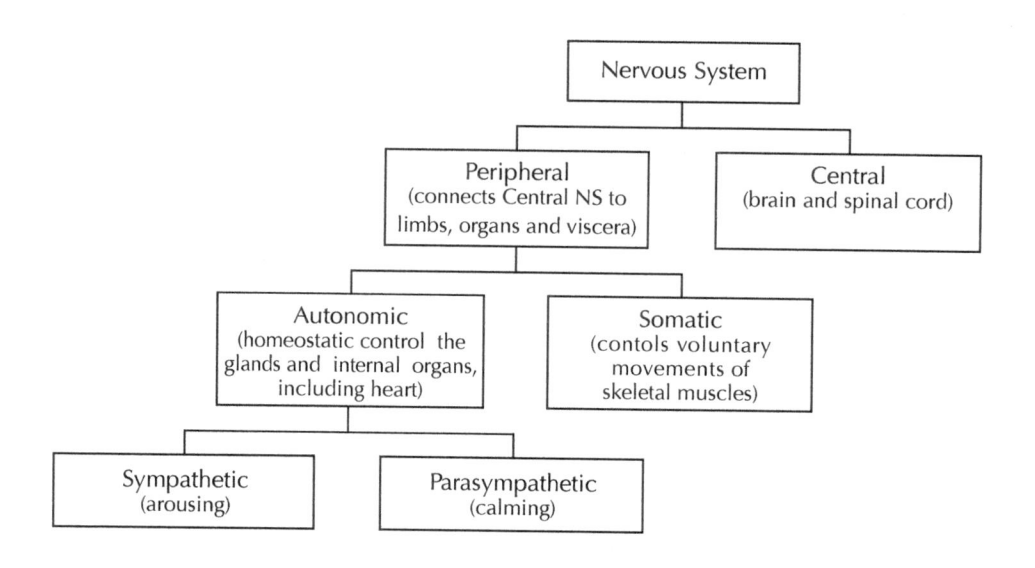

```
                        Nervous System
                       /              \
              Peripheral              Central
        (connects Central NS to    (brain and spinal cord)
        limbs, organs and viscera)
           /            \
    Autonomic          Somatic
  (homeostatic control the   (controls voluntary
   glands and internal organs,  movements of
       including heart)         skeletal muscles)
      /          \
 Sympathetic    Parasympathetic
  (arousing)      (calming)
```

DO ANIMALS HAVE EMOTIONS? *WE ARE ANIMALS!*

Dr. Jaak Panksepp is one of the leading neuroscientists in the world today. His work has focused on the nature of the basic emotional systems of the mammalian brain, with his most recent work devoted to analyzing the brain mechanisms that mediate separation distress and social bonding. His work is aimed at deepening and broadening our understanding of these systems biologically. His work leaves no doubt that animal emotions are the foundation of human emotions.

In *Affective Neuroscience: the Foundations of Human and Animal Emotions* (1998, pp. 246-7), Dr. Panksepp writes, "We are finally deciphering the ancient neurosymbolic processes that first led to nurturance and social attachments in the mammalian brain. Our understanding of these issues in the animal brain is impressive.... The working assumption is that the information obtained from animals will apply reasonably well to understanding basic emotional tendencies in humans."

Panksepp (2011) describes three levels of control over affective states, corresponding to our tri-brain evolutionary heritage.

Primary process emotions are sub-cortical, originating in the brainstem. These include such primitive affects as sensory stimulation, homeostatic needs of the body, and emotional action systems that embody primitive intentions.

Secondary process emotions, originating in the forebrain* and limbic system, are heavily shaped by learn-

---
* The most anterior region of the embryonic brain, or the segment of the adult brain that develops from this, including the cerebrum, thalamus, and hypothalamus.

ing in the form of early conditioning and social learning, most importantly the patterns developed in bonding and attachment. It is in the primitive, preconscious primary and secondary levels of emotion, that we are most like other animals. But then, that's the point, isn't it?! We *are* animals!

Tertiary process emotions are primarily neocortical. These are woven with thought, meaning, and judgment, though even these are guided by sub-cortical affects and learning. Emotional ruminations, as well as our attempts to self-regulate, and the intention to act sometimes referred to as "free will" are also primarily tertiary processes. This neocortical region gives humans their tremendous capacity for abstraction and cause-and-effect thinking. However, most psychological disorders do not begin at this level.

Psychological disorders or symptoms (including PTSD and many other diagnostic categories), have roots deep within the primary and secondary levels of affective experience. The core of many disorders is unregulated or dysregulated emotion circuits, activated in the brainstem and limbic system (primary and secondary levels of emotional process). The challenge is how to get the psychological healing to take hold at that level, which is difficult to access consciously and verbally. Clients may experience heightened arousal whenever they are in a human environment, activating defenses. A sense of alienation and difficulties in trusting other people, are almost universal features of complex forms of PTSD.

Moving a person from trauma to healing requires restructuring of emotional response. This must come in the form of new *experiences* that engage and soothe, or "regulate" this sensitive limbic region of the brain. The healing must engage and regulate primary and secondary process emotions. The book *A General Theory of Love* (Lewis et al., 2000) explains the neurological re-wiring that can happen within a bonded relationship. Limbic neuroplasticity—the remodeling of affective neural pathways and responses—requires three stages:

- limbic resonance, defined as a shared empathy in which two mammals become attuned to each other's inner states;
- limbic regulation, defined as reading each other's emotional cues, adjusting to each other and soothing or regulating the physiology of the other;
- limbic revision, defined as adaptation to a healthier template for future relationships

(Lewis et al., 2000; Siegel, 2010; Doidge, 2007).

> *"Because our minds seek one another through limbic resonance, because our physiologic rhythms answer to the call of limbic regulation, because we change one another's brains through limbic revision—what we do inside relationships matters more than any other aspect of human life."* (*A General Theory of Love*, Lewis et al., 2000, p. 192)

Limbic revision does not just change our feelings or ideas about relationship; it literally changes the brain and creates new neural pathways that can only be born of new experiences. One of the most exciting discoveries of the late twentieth century is that the neurons that make up our brain and nervous system are much more adaptable and regenerative than previously thought. Even the primary and secondary level neural pathways can essentially "rewire" themselves, given the right opportunities and conditions (Doidge, 2007). Neurons are uniquely designed to change in response to activity. Neural networks change in a use-dependent fashion. Chaotic experiences during sensitive times of a child's development create chaotic, dysfunctional neural organization that persists into adulthood; the good news is that neural systems will change for the better with dedicated amounts of focused repetition (Perry, 2008).

> *"A neural system cannot be changed without activating it, just as one cannot learn how to write by just hearing about [it]... without practicing."* (*The Neurosequential Model of Therapeutics*, Perry, 2008, p. 42)

> *"What has been wounded in relationship must, after all, be healed in relationship."* (*A Shining Affliction*, Rogers, 1996, p. 265)

SIMILARITIES IN HORSE AND HUMAN BRAINS

Can the working bond with the horse create such emotionally corrective experiences?

Research by Panksepp (1998) has proven that the limbic system is remarkably similar in humans and other mammals, enabling pair bonding, parenting behaviors, imprinting and enculturation of young, and everyday social community bonds. Horses keenly sense limbic activity and ANS arousal in others. Horses and humans are "highly social" by nature, a cornerstone of our long alliance (Grandin et al., 2009).

Highly social mammals need contact with others for their own neural regulation. In extreme circumstances the ANS signals fight-or-flight; during times of safety it can 'rest and digest.' For these extremes and all the states in between, social mammals attune to each other—for validation of concerns, reassurance and comfort. Belonging with, and counting on others, is essential for highly social mammals, whose brains rely on the regulating power of relationship (Lewis et al., 2000; Siegel, 2010). Without social connection the brain suffers.

Horses and humans share similarities in social structure as well. Wild horses live in small, family-based bands, sharing a wider range with hundreds of other bands that make up a herd (Grandin, 2009). This supports my direct experience and observation over many years facilitating horsemanship for the public, that horses have a vast relational memory. They readily distinguish dozens of clients, sometimes after only one distinct encounter, and may recognize them even years later.

Horses are prey animals, reading humans limbically at (physically) wider angles of view, better than humans can read them—with the human narrow field of view and an overdeveloped neocortex getting in the way (Grandin, 2005). Key facial expressions are universal to cultures throughout the world. This assures a limbic connection between therapist, client and horse; the client being particularly transparent when limbically connecting with the horse. This seems remarkable, since feelings are often expressed facially in milliseconds and fade almost immediately (Lewis et al., 2000).

Limbic similarity allows a person and a horse to form an evocative and memorable connection. The client experiences emotional regulation within a real-life working bond with the horse. The bond is not sentimental (though it may be full of feeling) nor is it a one-sided fantasy bond. It is a palpable bond of attention and respect that person and horse maintain. It enables working safely together on challenging, even risky tasks. *In truth, all tasks with a horse are risky when we lack such a connection!*

THE SIX KEYS TO RELATIONSHIP

The HEAL Six Keys to Relationship describe domains of affective and interpersonal functioning, relevant to horses and humans in relationships. The Keys help the practitioner keep the focus on the limbic interactions of client and horse. The domains are described in Figure 3, next page. The Six Keys are utilized in processing so the focus is on limbic and interpersonal processes, rather than procedural methods of horsemanship.

We've integrated an understanding of the identified neural circuits for major affective states—circuits that evoke the same archetypal behaviors (i.e., attempts to escape, distress vocalizations) in all mammals including humans. Panksepp has dubbed these "blue ribbon emotions," signifying these identified neural circuits with all capital letters (i.e., RAGE).

These primitive affective neural circuits are powerful, designed to drive key survival behaviors. Clients can observe horses in all six affective domains; in this their emotional lives are similar to our own. Being able to soothe and regulate the horse, and accept regulation from the horse, is essential to safety with the horses even in the simplest activities. Affective arousal is a bottom up process that influences feelings, thought and behavior. The Keys enable exploration of these affective domains in ways that are safely contained for human and horse.

Keys signify both access and responsibility. Barbara Rector, acknowledged as one of the grandmothers of EFPL, teaches the following promise, which we use with every client at HEAL: "*I agree to be responsible for myself physically, emotionally and spiritually.*" This is reinforced, and modeled, at all levels appropriate to the client's emotional development and physical ability. This pledge is an important part of the client's experience at HEAL.

The Six Keys to Relationship assist the clinician and client in exploring six different affective domains with the horse. This process illuminates client patterns, and helps them develop the tools for self-regulation within an actual, real-time relationship. The bond they develop with the horse is palpable, a practical working

Figure 3. The affective domains that are "HEAL's Six Keys to Relationship"

Affective Domain (KEY)	Blue Ribbon Neural Circuit; Associated behavior prime	Stage of horse relationship in EFPL
Key One Body Awareness	FEAR/sense of safety Primed for escape, freeze	*Beginning stage of EFPL* Self awareness, baselines, inner and outer; meeting and becoming acquainted; noticing resonance; choosing and being chosen. Insuring respect and trust; boundaries protect your reality; learning to calm a nervous horse. *Characterized by emotional resonance*
Key Two Boundaries	RAGE when trapped; Primed to fight	
Key Three Triggers–Defenses (Divided Self)	PANIC—separation anxiety; primed for frantic attempts to fit in; fear of rejection	*Middle stage of EFPL:* Figuring out dynamics of the relationship; muddling through friction and discomfort. Noticing and responding to disruptions in connection. Who is leading? Is the leader kind, fair? Balance of assertiveness and sensitivity; clear and congruent communication. *Characterized by emotional regulation*
Key Four Initiation–Assertiveness (Yin and Yang)	PLAY—rough and tumble, dominance hierarchy- who moves whom?	
Key Five Imagination (Deer Paths)	SEEKING—high drive state; primed to explore, investigate	*Culmination stage of EFPL* Performance and play based on practiced ability to read each other; Collaborating and co-creating with trust and enjoyment; feelings of belonging and connection, and accomplishment. *Characterized by emotional revision*
Key Six Interpersonal (The Social Brain) (Oxytocin-based nurturant circuits, Panksepp, 1998, p. 246)	CARE Circuits—pair and parent-child bonds, social standing; primed to protect and nurture	

bond in which human and horse *each look for, and look out for, the other*. Some clients may not feel deeply emotional toward the horse, yet they will still benefit from developing the bond by cultivating empathy and gaining awareness of their own mixed signals in relationship, which they can apply to the relationships that they do care about.

At the risk of oversimplification I have used the term CARE to include the social attachment aspects of all committed relationships. The term CARE refers most specifically to parentally focused oxytocin circuits; yet these circuits form the affective core for a wide variety of nurturant and pro-social behaviors, including some aspects of sexual pair bonding. CARE circuits are activated in males who learn nurturant behaviors, and Panksepp reports that, "… sexual activity can strengthen anti-aggressive, care-giving substrates in male brains" (1998, p. 246).

For most clients undergoing individual therapy or one of our time-limited groups, the experience follows a course with a beginning, a middle, and an end. The beginning stage is characterized by new awareness. The middle stage involves the work of relationship—how to be heard and respected in the ways we need and want. The horse wants the client to succeed in the relationship. Typically the ending stage of therapy can be filled with experiences that exceed the client's previous estimation of self, worth and the uplifting power of relationship. The facilitator must be skilled at helping the client bridge the learning to their human world. This is the power of limbic revision: *fragile but vivid* new neural pathways.

Author Temple Grandin, a hero in the world of animal welfare and science, and a highly accomplished individual who has autism, has also recognized the value of Panksepp's work. Her book, *Animals Make Us Human* (2009), advocates this rule for animal welfare:

> "Everyone who is responsible for animals—farmers, ranchers, zookeepers, and pet owners —needs a set of simple reliable guidelines... And the best guidelines we have are the core emotion systems in the brain. The rule is simple: don't stimulate RAGE, FEAR, and PANIC if you can help it; and do stimulate SEEKING and also PLAY." (p. 23)

Can we as humans learn something very important by implementing this principle in a relationship with a simple but powerful being? A being who is generous but also reactive. One who is noble, but also in some ways fragile. In other words, beings much like ourselves.

RESONANCE, REGULATION, REVISION: IN OUR CLIENTS' OWN WORDS

A replication of the HEAL 2006 pilot study (Shambo et al., 2010), was done in 2008 at HEAL. A thorough discussion of both the quantitative and qualitative data used in it can be found in Zasloff, (2009). In addition, in years 2008 through 2011 we collected qualitative data, using a semi-structured written interview from a total of 23 participants in PTSD groups at HEAL. There were 20 female and 3 male participants.[*] I have sorted responses into categories reflecting the stages of emotional healing identified by Lewis et al. (2000) in *A General Theory of Love*: 1) the client feeling *resonance* with the horse; 2) working things out including the need to *regulate* each other, and 3) accomplishment of a healthy and dynamic bond leads to *revision* of the old templates.

One participant's description captures all three themes:

> "Gypsy and I worked together almost exclusively the entire program. She showed me how to hold and focus my energy, responded to my learning to set boundaries and by the end of the program I've felt that we are partners in this dance of life. The experience began in joy and has ended in a gentle partnership."

---

[*] Informed consent to participate in the study was obtained from all participants (and guardian of youth participants). Study design and implementation approved by Lewis and Clark College Human Subjects Research Committee in 2008; the same design was implemented with oversight from HEAL Board of Directors in 2009, 2010 and 2011.

Resonance: Themes of "feeling seen, understood and valued"

"Feeling special."

"So calm, so relaxing, so in tune." "Calm, worth, loved."

"They [the horses] helped me in feeling that I had meaning."

"Beau was the horse I worked with and he really showed me that I was a 'worthy' person. Cause I have always been told that I was not worthy and would never amount to nothing."

"We bonded. Magic could read me like a book as well as I could read her."

"Was really a bonding experience and felt really the love and centered. I have made good boundaries and friends with Gem."

Regulation: Themes of "Working things out"

"To listen to the way my body is feeling and calming myself down. And about personal space and how important it really is."

"Grounding and balancing myself." "Getting out of my comfort zone."

"This has given me the courage to stand up for myself and defuse panic attacks, set boundaries and bond—with people too."

"It has taught me to set good boundaries, and not be scared."

"Gem was able to reflect to me when my energies weren't congruent. She flowed effortlessly when I was 'in tune' with my body. I couldn't have done it without her."

"I learned to calm myself before interacting with others. Make sure people understand my personal space and I respect others' space. I learned to trust others who respect my space."

Revision: Themes of "Emotional competency with the horse; skills taken into life"

"The ability to be assertive with something so much larger than myself, to firmly set boundaries and to feel confident within myself. I am more positive about my future and more decisive in my actions than I was previously."

"The assertiveness skills are something that are huge things for me. Now I'm really able to spread my self-preservation wings."

"I am more aware of being grounded in all aspects of my life often times it's the awareness that I'm too much in my head instead of my body but I hope one day I'll be able to feel comfortable in my body at all times."

"Total impact: I have feelings, a voice, and more tools to use."

"I find myself using all I have learned in very stressful situations, and now understand better how to deal with those moments."

"I am more open and honest, communicate and learn the other persons' boundaries, it's a more open way to relate to that person."

EFPL VIGNETTES ILLUSTRATE THE SIX KEY PROGRESSION

In the next six chapters, we follow the progress of two different clients who have participated in therapeutic experiences at the HEAL Ranch. I have selected these vignettes from actual client sessions, to represent a "typical" progression through a course of therapy, which is very different for these two clients. In both cases it is possible to identify the beginning, middle and end phase of the therapeutic experience. Linda was an adult client who came regularly for individual therapy over a two-year period. Tina was a young adolescent who participated in a diagnosis-specific, time-limited group. Both are survivors of repeated childhood trauma.

EFPL Practitioner's Note: Linda

Linda, age thirty-seven, was recently divorced from a five-year marriage she described as emotionally cold. She had not had previous therapy. Though she was professionally successful she was largely unable to cultivate intimate involvement or close friendships in either her personal or professional life. Previous boyfriends and her ex-husband were like strangers who used her body in return for a security that Linda craved but could never feel. Linda was experiencing increasing depression and relentless worry. She felt very removed from others. Therapy was a last resort, which she had never tried. Therapy with a horse? Linda decided to come to HEAL for EFPL sessions, although it was over an hour from her home.

Linda entered individual therapy and we started with an assessment and history. In the beginning Linda was largely uneducated about mental health effects stemming from traumatic experiences long past. Her presenting condition was that she felt desperately unhappy and isolated, yet unable to risk close relationships. Assessment instruments revealed that depression and anxiety were in the severe range. The character of her symptoms, combined with her past history, fit the criteria for chronic PTSD. Lack of ability to cope with stress was putting her health at risk, impacting her career. Linda's therapeutic work at HEAL included office-based sessions as well as EFPL sessions; I also referred her to other providers for a medication consult and body therapy.

Linda's therapy focused on relieving somatic symptoms by learning to self-regulate arousal, and changing longstanding patterns of relationship that were shaped by dysfunction. Both of these goals were well served through the EFPL, along with more conventional strategies.

EFPL Practitioner's Note: Tina

Tina was a participant in an adolescent group PTSD program, which met during one summer for seven sessions (weekly) of three hours per session. Tina was fourteen years old, and one of five girls who participated in that group. All were referred by a local community mental health agency. Tina was waif-like and withdrawn, appearing two years younger than her given age and very thin.

At the time of her treatment Tina's symptoms were acute and overlapped with the developmental demands of an intensely dynamic life stage—puberty. Her sense of safety and worth seriously compromised by abuse, Tina lacked the building blocks for neurosequential personality development and social success. Tina was falling behind her peers in many ways. The goal of our group treatment was to provide targeted, vivid experiences that would readily internalize as resources and skills.

In the PTSD groups my *treatment contract* is with the *agency* that contracts me to provide a service. In this case it was the local Community Mental Health Center, Cascade Mental Health Care in Chehalis, WA. Technically we provide a "learning" intervention (EFL), coordinating our treatment with the primary therapist from the agency. Still, the PTSD groups demand a high level of professional experience, and are challenging to conduct. At times particular clients may become dissociative, helpless and frightened, or angry. This emotion easily becomes contagious to other group members and the horses. It is important to respond to the client in intense emotional distress in ways that soothe as well as contain, allowing the client a new experience. The horse can be an important ally in this containment.

Bonding within the Herd

Horses possess the natural instinct to regulate other herd members. Historically, we as humans have paid attention to the dominance hierarchy within a horse band. Dominance is often used in forcing horses to submit to human use, a style of training that is not suitable for EFPL. The stabilizing matrix of bonding and regulating behaviors plays an even more important role in keeping the herd together, alive and in balance. *Bonding and regulating behaviors* are also the most powerful influences used by expert horsemen and women. Study horses in their relationships with each other and you will see that they are limbically purposeful, precise and individualized in their responses to other horses, and to humans as well given the right conditions. These are the very conditions we create for effective EFPL in the HEAL Model, by using the Six Keys to Relationship.

Chapter Three

The First Key: Body-Centered Awareness

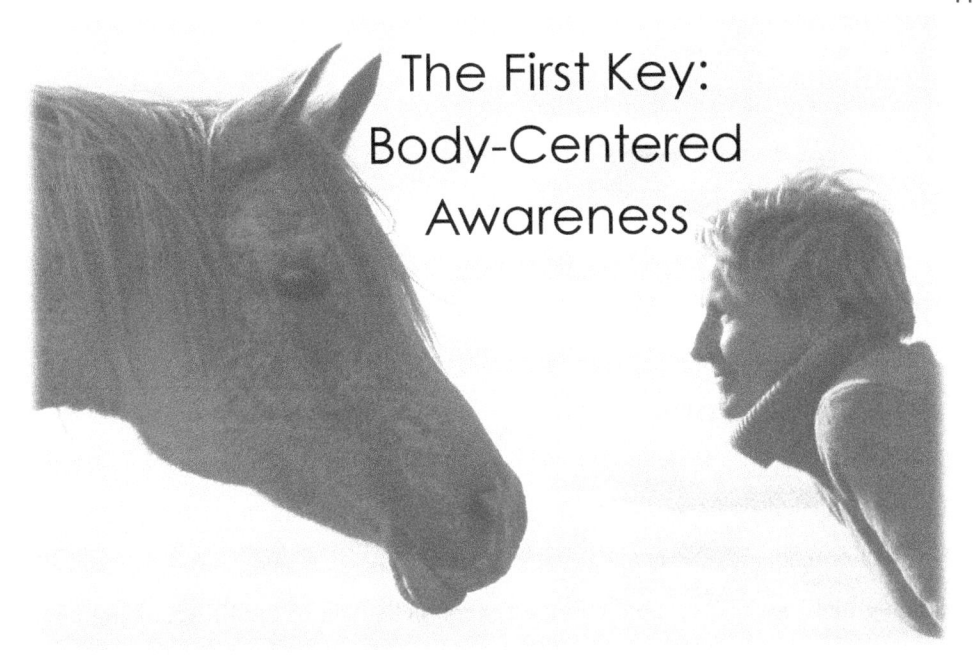

"Neural networks throughout the interior of the body, including those surrounding the intestines and heart, send complex sensory input to the skull-based brain. Such input from the body forms a vital source of intuition and powerfully influences reasoning and the way we create meaning in our lives."

Dr. Daniel Siegel
Mindsight

THERAPEUTIC STRATEGY IN KEY ONE: BODY-CENTERED AWARENESS

Wounded, mistrustful people and horses often really "*get*" each other. Trauma and other types of significant stress and unresolved history alter the neural pathways, memory storage and the electrochemical operations of the brain and ANS. Experiencing the violation and horror of trauma, humans can become like prey animals, ready to run, or in a constant state of hypervigilance or mistrust. Fight, flight or freeze. Trauma aside, neural patterns for feeling states may be "turned off" or set on "overdrive" for a variety of reasons, including living in the unnatural conditions of modern life.

Using Key One, the therapist helps the client to become mindful of basic somatic sensations; to be able to track these and report on them with specificity and neutrality. Mindfulness is noticing, without justification, defense or apology. We want to help the client notice autonomic signs such as breathing and heartbeat, and be able to track and report arousal as it changes. This may be challenging for clients with a trauma background. Some clients will feel quite numb, avoidant of feelings. Other clients may have profound experiences of heart-pounding panic or exhausting hypervigilance. Beneath these defensive symptoms, tuning in to somatic sensation can uncover overwhelming memories of horror, terror and loss.

FEAR is one of the most ancient emotional energies shared by horses and humans, for good reason. FEAR is, according to Panksepp, "An aversive state of the nervous system, characterized by apprehensive worry, general nervousness and tension, *which tells creatures that their safety is threatened* [emphasis added]," (1998, P. 207). FEAR can be an important messenger, even an ally when working with horses. But excessive FEAR can paralyze and hold a person or horse hostage, unable to live a productive life under safe conditions. Conversely, the adrenaline of FEAR can become addictive, leading to excessive risk or impulsive behavior.

The neural circuit of FEAR primes the animal or human for escape and avoidance behaviors. In truth, the symptoms of PTSD reflect a FEAR system that was bombarded and overwhelmed, leaving lasting neural pathways of alarm that include reactive, brainstem-driven reactions. Therapeutic efforts must activate the neural systems that mediate that particular client's symptoms, and a high percentage of our clients will suffer with anxiety. Chronic high anxious arousal points to the general activation of the FEAR neural network that has become patterned on threat. An important clinical task is to help clients distinguish between productive and non-productive FEAR states. This can't be accomplished until the client learns how to gauge their somatic signs and stay in touch with their level of autonomic arousal.

Horses can become difficult to work with, or even dangerously reactive (being a creature of flight) when they are afraid. It will be important to coach the client in calming the horse and building its trust. When the horse is slightly nervous, the client can check their own body activation and calm themselves through breathing and grounding. The most important task of Key One is for the client to begin consciously managing arousal in self and horse. It is this dual regulation that develops the ability to modulate energy, which has a tremendously empowering effect on the client and the development of the EFPL experience.

Within EFPL, we can treat FEAR (in all of its various costumes) thoughtfully, and by this create safety and trust with the horse. With Key One the therapist and client turn their attention to noticing both the client's, and the horse's, overall level of activation or arousal. The client is encouraged to notice sensations with specificity (for example, the client can track overall excitement/arousal/activation on a scale of 0-10, or track the intensity of specific sensations). The therapist will help the client stay attuned to relatively subtle somatic sensations, and track these sensations as the client meets and begins interacting with a horse or horses.

In the process of meeting the horses and simple introductory interactions with them the therapist develops a rapport with the client for talking about body sensations and feeling states. The length of time to develop this rapport varies greatly from client to client, being influenced by many factors. Some clients may be afraid or cautious of horses; others may feel excited or confident. The therapist is able to relate a healthy level of body awareness to the client's developing competence with the horse.

In the book *The Body Remembers,* author Babette Rothschild (2000, p. 101) describes body awareness as both *precise* and *subjective*. Most sensations are clearly *subjective*—for instance the client may report, while with a particular horse, a sensation of heaviness in the heart, or a feeling that she wants to laugh. Some sensations have a subjective and objective component. For example, a person may feel that their heart rate is very high. Clients can monitor heart rate in real time by feeling their pulse (simple calculation to beats per minute). Body-centered awareness is a combined awareness of signals from within as well as signals from the immediate environment (present moment, here and now).

Horsemanship *expands* body awareness from an isolated, strictly internal state to a balanced awareness of the body in its immediate environment, *now*. The HEAL Model begins with gentle body mindfulness in preparation for meeting the horses. In Key One *sense of safety, subjectively precise body awareness, and mindful noticing of self and environment* are the topics of focus. The therapeutic task is to develop awareness of this inner platform, this inner hub of awareness and knowing, an inner compass, which is available to the client.

The horses will be aware of the client's somatic signs such as breath, muscle tension and heart rate. This gives human and horse an interface in which each begins "feeling" the other. In general, the horses will not overreact to the client's somatic state, as long as they have a trusted facilitator anchoring the situation. Gentle horses have a broad tolerance for human states of consciousness, though they have distinct reactions to different clients. Start where your client is. Give a manageable amount of information presented in a way that's relevant to them, and support them to use the information as they observe and interact with the horses.

Youth and adult clients can be educated about the mind-body system, and mindfulness-based stress reduction strategies. It is best to keep such information simple: the goal is to get the client to tune in to their own signs of arousal in a gentle, curious manner. There is not a "right way" for the client to begin noticing their feeling-based implicit navigation system.

Proper abdominal breathing is an essential skill for interacting with horses. It is quite natural and most clients will not find it difficult to learn. However, some clients may experience emotional flooding, panic, or other somatic symptoms. The clinician should help the client move through these reactions to gently support more relaxed and adaptive breathing. Responsive energy modulation occurs within the client, and between client and horse.

Key One can be likened to a Master Key, because successful use of all the other keys depends upon Key One. The client becomes more aware of the feeling hub of awareness. By attending to and cultivating Body-Centered Awareness, the therapist helps client develop the body as a gauge and a resource. The client will return to this Key One frequently, to appraise and adjust their use of the other Keys.

TYPICAL EFPL ACTIVITIES FOR KEY ONE

Meeting the Herd, or introducing the horses, patterns a protocol for coming together moments that become a positive relationship practice. Safety instruction appropriate to the type of client(s) being served should be provided, with an emphasis on using their own "inner compass" as an important gauge of safety for themselves and the horse at all times. The safety instruction should emphasize care for the horse's feelings and humane training as the preferred course (some clients may have experienced the horse as object in other settings).

Choose a way to introduce the horses that is appropriate to the client's stage of development, their reasons for being in therapy, level of defense with the therapist, as well as their level of cognitive functioning. For instance, with an adult client I may provide a cognitive explanation of the tri-brain, ANS and neural pathways. With others (especially younger clients) we may just have a little chat about breathing, excitement or nervousness, and how they notice that in themselves, on the way out to the stables or pasture.

When the client is meeting more than one horse, it is often convenient to observe them individually in small paddocks. It's fascinating to find out how each client perceives the different horses (the observations range from tuned out, to astute, to highly intuitive). With returning clients, I inspire the practice of seeing something new in the horse each day, to really *look*. By being mindful of how we shape the client's meeting the horse or horses on a particular day, we begin to help the client shape new limbic patterns for relational experience.

Once safety is established, some of the basic parameters of mammal to mammal friendship can be explored. Help the client be relaxed and gentle in mind and in body language. Recognize that body language is like a conversation that flows between a person and the horse. Discover if the horse trusts/ enjoys touch. Can you touch the horse's whole body? Help the client learn to assess the horse's level of arousal, and notice what they notice. Friends listen to each other, and are honest with each other. Friendship is a feeling, sensing *process*.

Look for opportunities to have the client "synch" their breathing with the horse, exploring touch, close physical contact, and experience the safety and influence zones around the horse's body. There will be opportunities to have the client learn to calm the horse when it is slightly nervous; conversely there will be times when the horse becomes bored or inattentive, in ways that are not safe as well. It is all about balance.

Safety instruction and comfort in touching the horse and moving around their body safely are an important part of the early stage of therapy and the developing body awareness. Clients vary greatly in their capacity to be responsible for their own safety, and when the client cannot be responsible the practitioner MUST be responsible. *The client's capacity for safe responding can change very quickly during EFPL, as can the horse's energy and attention.*

Allow plenty of time for the client's experience, and for the horse to lead. Be prepared to follow process and work with what the horse is showing and how the client is reacting. For instance, in the pen with a loose horse, it may take time for the horse to approach. The horse may meander before approaching the client (the client may experience disappointment or worry). The EFPL facilitator should be aware of and prepared to follow the limbic signals between human client and horse.

Horse and music therapies overlap in very synergistic ways in the exploration of Key One. Patterned repetitive sensory input will predictably influence brainstem neural systems into smoother, more functional regulation. An introductory stroking/touching/grooming session often benefits from music in the background. Music can be used effectively with clients of any age as they learn to walk beside the horse in early leading activities. Adults and children benefit from relaxing music played during therapeutic horse sessions. This is especially true for clients that have such high chronic arousal that soothing the brainstem is an issue of first concern, before skill building or stretching emotional tolerance.

Teaching clients to consciously use their breath for calming (emphasize out breath), or the in-breath for raising energy, gives them an especially powerful way to influence themselves and the horse for the positive in almost any situation. A balanced state created by rhythmic abdominal breathing will almost always cause the horse to relax, as horses do among themselves when they are at rest. Highly aroused or anxious clients find it extremely soothing to walk and trot with the horse, using the in breath to signal the upward (walk to trot) transitions, out-breath for down (trot to walk) transitions. This will begin to create the limbic bond as the horse becomes more alert to what the person is doing, and the person needs to adjust themselves to the horse.

✒ EFPL FACILITATION TOPIC ✒
My Well-Being Agreement

"My name is _____ and I agree to be responsible for myself physically, emotionally and spiritually ... and in this way contribute to the safety and learning of the group" [or myself and others, this marriage, my family etc. as appropriate to therapeutic situation].

This self-contract, articulated by Barbara Rector in her book *Adventures in Awareness* (2005, p. 87), is a perfect way to open therapy with horses, even for children. *EFPL is riskier than traditional office-based therapy; the client has recognized this by signing a liability waiver.* We want to empower the client with their own sense of good judgment and an ability to consciously use accurate feelings as a help in navigating social-emotional situations.

Taking Responsibility for What?

In EFPL a primary factor is the human self-awareness of excitement, arousal or internal activation. By teaching the HEAL Keys you will be helping clients learn how to sort and manage arousal of various social-emotional 'flavors.' The following practice technique (or a client-friendly version thereof) will prove useful in supporting clients to learn the specific ways in which they can become responsible for their own feelings and responses.

Figure 4. The 0-10 point arousal scale

Positive Arousal Comfortable	Negative Arousal Uncomfortable	
		Increased sensation Emotional reactivity Hypervigilance Intrusive imagery Disorganized cognitive processing
Feelings	**Feelings**	**Hyperarousal Zone (over 10)**
Ecstatic	Rage	10
Excited	Fear	9
Euphoric	Angry	8
Happy	Irritated	7
Eager	Anxious	
	Edgy	**Window of Tolerance** 6
		Optimal Arousal Zone 5
		4
		3
Content	Bored	2
Calm	Listless	
Meditative	Numb	1
Peaceful	Unfeeling	0
Restful	Uncaring	
		Hypoarousal Zone (under 10)
		Relative absence of sensation Numbing of emotions Disabled cognitive processing Reduced physical movement

Metaphors, such as the thermometer, help the client understand arousal as a gauge for their own reactions. Help them notice how the horse responds as human arousal fluctuates, and how the horse's arousal level changes too.

Zones of Arousal from *Trauma and the Body: A Sensorimotor Approach to Psychotherapy*, by Pat Ogden, Kekuni Minton, and Clare Pain (2006). Used with permission.

❧ EFPL FACILITATION TOPIC ☙
The 10 Point Arousal Scale

Reference Figure 4: The 10 Point Arousal Scale

0 = no sensation, numb or shut down (negative valence); low numbers such as 1-2 can be deeply peaceful (positive valence).

10 = so aroused that the body must move (alternatively the person may dissociate from feeling). Jittery, pacing, looking about, tapping hand or foot, compulsively checking messages— these are examples of anxious arousal (negative valence). Shouting, interrupting, striking fist on table—are examples of angry arousal (negative valence). Exclamations of happiness, pressing hands together, playful action—are all examples of happy, hopeful, or joyful arousal (positive valence).

Clients' awareness of arousal may be explored starting with the following questions.

1. How high or low is your level of arousal (or "activation") right now? (arousal level)
2. Is the arousal you have comfortable or not? Enjoyable or unpleasant? Mixed? (valence)
3. What sensations help you recognize this arousal? (report specific sensations)
4. Is the number changing as we talk about it?

The client's attention should be directed specifically to autonomic arousal affecting heart rate, respiration, sweating, viscera (i.e., butterflies in stomach etc.), muscle tension, pupil dilation, facial muscles and eye movements. Arousal can be positive or negative; this is referred to as its *valence*. Is it comfortable or not? Clients should recognize that arousal comes from pleasant as well as unpleasant feelings. High positive arousal causes cognitive distortion and can lead to impulsive behavior, just as negative arousal does. Beware of anything over 7.5, on this 0-10 point scale!

❧ EFPL FACILITATION TOPIC ☙
Mindfulness Breathing

Mindfulness breathing essentially involves focusing your mind on your breath, in the present, without judging yourself. Research suggests that mindfulness breathing may improve mood, decrease stress, and boost immune function.

How to Try Mindfulness Breathing

1. It is helpful to use a small clock or timer. Start with 5-10 minutes, increasing to 20 or 30 minutes as you get comfortable. It works well to have a regular time of day, such as just after rising or at night before going to bed.

2. Find a quiet and comfortable place. Sit in a chair or on the floor with your head, neck and back straight but not stiff. Don't lean or slump, but do sit naturally.

3. Try to put aside all thoughts of the past and the future and stay in the present.

4. Become aware of your breathing, focusing on the sensation of air moving in and out of your body as you breathe. Feel your belly rise and fall, the air enter your nostrils and leave your mouth. Pay attention to the way each breath changes and is different.

5. Watch every thought come and go, whether it is a worry, fear, anxiety or hope. When thoughts come up in your mind, don't ignore or suppress them but simply note them, remain calm and use your breathing as an anchor.

6. If you find yourself getting carried away in your thoughts, observe where your mind went off to, without judging, and simply return to your breathing. Remember not to be hard on yourself if this happens.

7. As the time comes to a close, sit for a minute or two, becoming aware of where you are.

EFPL HORSE ACTIVITY
Meeting the Herd: A bottom up process of discovery

- The horses can be introduced in any safe and logical way that serves the general direction that you have chosen for the EFPL.

- The client should be prepared by assisting them to adopt a mindful state, tuned in to autonomic signs such as heart rate, breathing, and muscle tension. The story-making cortex should be quieted to allow for a bottom-up process of discovery.

- For adults, and some younger people, in the first session it is not uncommon for me to have the horses in individual outdoor paddocks. However depending on the weather and time of year clients might meet the horses in stalls. For some purposes, observation of the herd in a pasture makes a better first step than meeting the herd members individually.

- With young clients, and often in groups, the horse may be held on a lead line to create a more engaged meeting, and one with more structure and safety. This is the most structured way of introducing the client to the horse.

- Herd observation is a valuable exercise that does not involve meeting the herd per se, since the horses will usually remain engaged in their own activities and energetically connected to each other. Observing the herd provides opportunity for valuable discussion as clients point out and interpret relational interactions.

- As clients continue in therapy they will meet the herd in many different settings, for instance out in different pastures as a group or in pairs. When "meeting moments" are practiced mindfully they become a powerful relationship practice. This starts with being mindful of one's own state, then extending mindful observance and openness to the other that we are meeting.

- Careful listening to the client's narrative about different horses and their reaction to meeting them, will reveal a lot about the client's inner world, and degree of openness. Varying degrees of valid intuition, as well as projection, will be revealed and may be explored, or simply noted.

- Telling the client "about" the horses is not preferred. Telling tends to draw the client into the cognitive, judgment making mind—thinking about the horse instead of relating to the horse. Allowing feelings to become too literal is usually not helpful. The therapist helps the client sense her or himself first, then the horse, simply noticing changes.

MORE ABOUT KEY ONE: Body Centered Awareness

HRV and breathing-based biofeedback

At HEAL we often compare the horses to biofeedback, because they are so responsive to the autonomic signs in other mammals, including humans. Exploration of the client's breathing patterns, and intentional use of the breath to calm and communicate with the horse, are woven into the beginning phase of EFPL. Some clients, particularly adults with a long history of incorrect breathing, find biofeedback helpful. We keep a selection of hand-held and computer-based biofeedback instruments available for clients to try. The objective verification of ANS coherence offered by these devices helps clients gain confidence in their body as a resource— for their work with the horses, their relationship with other humans, and ultimately for their recovery and growth.

Heart rate variability (HRV) is a measure of vitality and resilience of a mammal's biological system, a measure that has received research attention in both human and horse research. It has been proposed by some researchers that HRV in humans may somehow be sensed by horses (Mistral, 2005). According to Reiner (2008, p. 58), "Short and long-term stress reactions and disorders associated with increased sympathetic activity typically involve a decrease in HRV/RSA [retinal sinus arrhythmia]. The literature corroborates the relationship between low HRV/RSA and numerous psychiatric and medical conditions..." (Cited on David Young's website www.HRVresearch.com)

For more information about breathing-based biofeedback that can be helpful in stress reduction and mindfulness instruction, the following websites have been good resources for our clients: www.stresseraser.com/science-of-the-stresseraser and www.heartmath.org.

KEY ONE Vignette
Linda—Beginning stage of individual EFPL

Linda knew how to ignore her body and the feelings locked up inside. She was physically strong, a runner who worked out at the gym several times a week. Yet, she had trouble with the breathing practice I assigned as homework—5 minutes of mindfulness breathing per day. It made her uncomfortable: first impatient, then a sense of panic—and she had difficulty sticking to it.

Her beginning sessions in EFPL gave us opportunities to explore Linda's breathing and arousal patterns. Meeting the herd became a mindfulness practice in itself, as Linda learned to find her baseline first, then spend several minutes viewing the horses and noticing changes in herself. Consistently, Linda found that this breathing practice felt safer to her while she was with the horses (rather than at home where she was more likely to feel "stressed out"). In particular, she liked striding along in rhythm with a horse, joined by a leadline, on the lanes and pastures of the HEAL Ranch. She learned to initiate an energetic connection with the horse, by varying her speed. She and the horse had to watch each other, and think, to stay in synch together.

Part of Linda remained stiff and reserved, even with the horses. She mostly navigated by the cognitive power that once served her so well in her professional life. The horses tended to move away when Linda explored close body contact or approached them at liberty. Linda's "normal" was a high level of anxious arousal, which was exhausting her—her body was on permanent "false alarm." And the horses could feel it.

During one session early in Linda's work at HEAL, Linda entered the arena where our three oldest horses were passing a hot afternoon. When none of them approached, Linda concluded she was beyond help. Her hands in fists, she slumped against the fence and banged her fist on it. A long moment passed. I waited. Frieda, the lead mare, approached and blew softly on Linda's cheek. She held her head close to Linda's upper back, whiskers touching, and breathed in and out rhythmically. Linda let out a huge sigh, her shoulders shaking. The other horses had moved in closer. Their bodies blocked my view, and they held this stance as Linda's tears subsided into huge releases of held breath.

Horses have an instinct to provide regulation and comfort to herd members in distress. Interacting with each other, they sense the breath—deep, slow breathing signals relaxation and well being; shallow, fast breathing means danger or discomfort. They exchange information through the breath. And horses are capable of collective action in the service of another herd member. In this case that herd member was Linda.

More about Linda in Chapter 5 …

Anchors

Anchors are positive associations that help your participant remember their strengths, and have faith in themselves and their world. These may be real people from their past (i.e. a grandmother who was always benevolent and caring, a teacher who believed in them). Animals often serve as important anchors (your own therapy horses will begin to serve as anchors for the people who come to learn from you). Special spots in nature, a personal relationship with God, or human or animal spirit guides can all be anchors for the participants' psyche in moments of stress and arousal.

Healthy people have a wealth of anchors and show great flexibility in using these to help modulate intensely emotional experiences. Always notice what inner resources participants talk about or seem to rely on as they speak about themselves. You can help a participant establish these anchors by asking about them directly, or by activities that you use as opening exercises, and by questions such as "What helped you get through that?"

When the client has a noticeable lack of positive associations, especially coupled with poor ability to self-modulate emotion, this should be a focus of therapy from the outset.

Bottom up vs. Top Down

Figure 5, Nested hierarchies of control within the brain, provides a schematic summary of the hierarchical bottom-up and top-down (circular) causation that is proposed to operate in every primal emotional system of the brain.

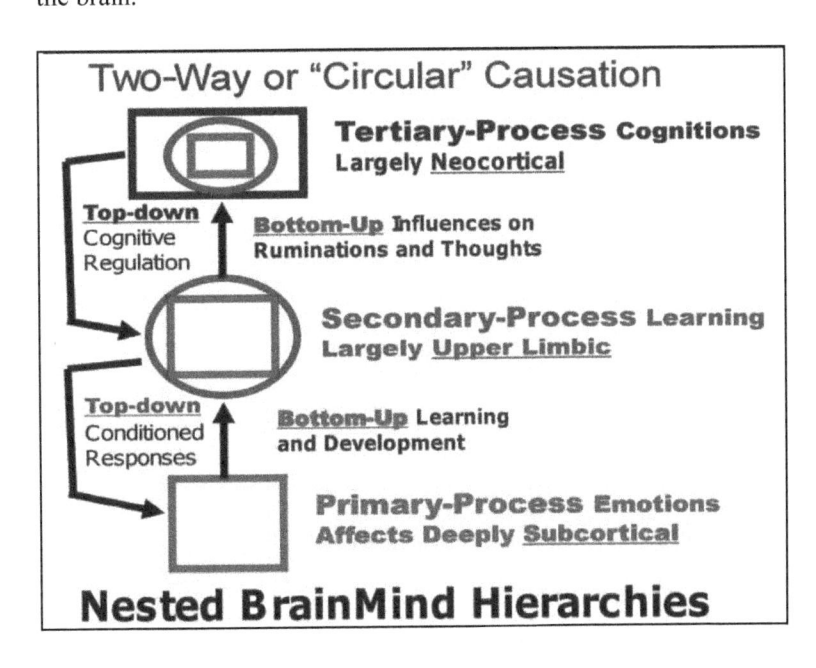

Figure 5. Nested hierarchies of control within the brain.

From: *Cross-Species Affective Neuroscience Decoding of the Primal Affective Experiences of Humans and Related Animals*, By Jaak Panksepp. Used with author's permission.
Published by PLoS ONE, www.plosone.org 6 August 2011, Volume 6 Issue 8 | e21236

Chapter Four

The Second Key: Boundaries

"In each social context, you choose your comfort zone and broadcast it to others with body language—with gestures, eye contact, posture, facial expression and how you listen. If your space is violated you may feel uncomfortable, threatened or upset."

Sandra and Matthew Blakeslee
The Body Has A Mind of Its Own

THERAPEUTIC STRATEGY IN KEY TWO: BOUNDARIES

Musician Cole Porter wrote the quintessential cowboy song in 1934. *Don't Fence Me In* described an enviable existence where no physical boundaries suppressed the cowboy's adventurous spirit. The song also suggests a mental condition that flourished on that wide open plain. Accompanied by his "cayuse," the cowboy resisted definition by anyone else's standards. He embraced his independence, his personal reality. This is freedom, right? Or is it loneliness?

Fences define areas of ownership and responsibility. A fence is a boundary. Though not a visible fence, boundaries are the membranes between oneself and others that facilitate relational freedom and closeness. Boundaries are a fundamental mammalian dignity, protecting individuality and personal space. They are energetic and psychological in nature. We explore boundaries in Key Two.

Using Key Two, the therapist assists the client in greater awareness of their own personal space bubble, noticing its unique characteristics, and the horse's space bubble too. It is important to connect the sensing of boundaries to the increase (or decrease) in arousal and specific sensations. Fluctuations in autonomic arousal are part of the body's involuntary reaction to the proximity or approach of others—person or horse. The autonomic nervous system (ANS), in addition to its multifaceted homeostasis function, also mediates the physiological cues for social engagement, trust and intimacy (Porges, 2011, p. 149).

Boundary intrusions, discrepancies or outright disputes are a common cause of negative emotional arousal, engaging the limbic neural circuit called RAGE. What is the relationship of boundaries to the RAGE circuit? The role of RAGE is to mobilize and direct all available energy to physical defense of self or offspring—in other words, RAGE may have significant inputs from FEAR/PANIC circuits (Panksepp, 1998, P 194). RAGE primes the behavior of survival fighting— affective attack—the all out struggle for life when it is threatened and escape is not possible.

Not all acts of aggression are threat-related; and not all acts of aggression stem from the RAGE circuit. Aggressive posturing and small punishments (a well-placed bite) communicate and reinforce social status in a horse herd (or between horse and human). Mating rights and sexual posturing involve aggression and conflict that are not properly of the RAGE circuit. A frustrated SEEKING circuit can also produce aggression. And so, while RAGE is not always the cause of aggression, the answer to aggression from another is always clear, strong boundaries.

Horses, being herbivores, are non-aggressive creatures and in general prefer flight to attack, but they will fight when cornered or trapped by a predator. However, it is common to see them using small acts of aggression to enforce boundaries within the herd, or to communicate boundary intrusion to a human. For instance, even a generally well-trained horse might defend itself against rough use of the curry, or the discomfort of girth tightening, with a nip. Boundaries are usually resolved very quickly in the herd, often based on the herd "pecking order," which is maintained with threats and posturing much more often than by inflicting actual pain and injury.

Boundaries and proximity are the most concrete expressions of respect and safety among horses. For a client who has just learned a little about noticing the nervous arousal in their own body, boundary practice with the horse will deepen the client's experience of their own arousal patterns. Healthy management of boundaries is one of the ways to help a nervous horse settle down. These are all reasons to explore boundaries early in the course of EFPL therapy. Boundaries permeate all levels of relationship, from appropriate versus inappropriate touch, to who is responsible for what household chores. Survivors of abuse and dysfunction within relationship often have seriously flawed templates for interpersonal boundaries.

Boundaries are for taking care of yourself, not for controlling or manipulating others (including the horse). Healthy boundaries create safety and protection, while allowing the stimulation of contact and differentiation. Rigid boundaries create walls and sometimes, isolation. Though boundaries are central to a successful life, healthy boundaries are impossible to develop if not experienced first in the primary relationships that shape the limbic landscape.

Practice with boundaries is essential to building new templates for relationship. Boundaries constantly change, and involve trust, nuance, and sensitivity. Because horses have a natural language of spatial relationship, and unique ability to sense both arousal and intent in human beings, they have tremendous potential to support relational boundary exploration in the therapeutic setting. Through work with horses, clients learn the importance of risking abandonment to set boundaries, that they are always part of the herd, and that they are liked and accepted more when boundaries are in place. The "cayuse" remains an excellent partner for exploring the freedom and connection found in boundaries.

In EFPL we pay attention to the sense of connection that healthy boundaries allow. For example, when a loose horse does not wish to be approached, we may coach the client to explore the "hang out distance" where they can be in contact, without making a demand on the horse. In almost every case, a horse who feels respected in this manner usually decides to meet and greet the human who offered, but did not push, connection.

It is not only trauma survivors who lack healthy templates and examples for boundaries. Our culture promotes enmeshed, even infantile, pictures of intimacy and belonging. So it is very productive to return to the grounded and concrete examples given by nature as we develop a peaceable and productive relationship with the horse. Lavender says, (2006, p.4) "Part of [the horse's] majesty is the horse possessing the innate ability to function within a herd or collective as well as maintain their individual 'horse-anality'… the horse has the ability to be an individual and Join-Up with other(s) at the same time while neither stance diminishes the other. Few humans in relationships seem to be able to make this claim."

New neural pathways that come from experiences of successful boundary negotiation with a half ton animal will be invaluable as the therapist supports the client in making bridges to human environments. Boundaries that have to do with power, responsibility and communication will be even more complex and variable in the human world than they are in a horse-human relationship, but there will be commonalities: how it feels to stand your ground, how acceptable it feels to simply request that someone back up a step, or the difference between a hard boundary and a soft boundary.

A common, though often unrecognized belief is that if boundaries are set, abandonment will follow. This is a classic childhood fear that can leak into adulthood. Pleasing and appeasing behaviors are created from a state of fear that when limits are set love will disappear. Even adults can feel guilty setting limits, believing that if someone simply likes them, respect and love will logically follow. On the contrary, *real friendship, love and connectedness thrive only if respect and safety come first*. And because respect and safety come first, boundaries must be maintained—this is another Key for our client's toolbox. A Key tool during EFPL therapy, and hopefully for a lifetime. Boundaries, like a healthy garden, are most productive when regularly tended. Boundaries are the flip side of connection; and horses are masterful at teaching both.

TYPICAL EFPL ACTIVITIES FOR EXPLORING KEY TWO

Working with youth or adult clients individually or in groups, I often deliver key information about boundary sensing via human-to-human demonstration. This can be very powerful and should be facilitated with sensitivity and respect. By approaching the client and having them approach me, I can help them learn to sense how their own arousal changes in response to the proximity of others.

Building on this, I demonstrate methods of signaling their boundaries to the horses they will soon be interacting with. Clients gain confidence in noticing the small signs of arousal in others—a person or a horse. And clients learn how to modulate the rate of approaching, and to modulate their own arousal as they approach—a more nuanced approach. An essential skill useful for approaching a shy horse is what my mentor Linda Kohanov (2007) describes as the "rock back and sigh" maneuver. This means to take at least a half step back off the boundary, and take steps to lower one's own arousal (as the approacher). Steps to lower arousal include an out breath, grounding/anchoring thoughts, and appreciative intentions such as being patient with the horse. During the demonstration clients can also be taught how to handle a boundary tool such as a training stick or a short whip, which may be needed in some situations.

By taking time to explore how it feels to approach and be approached, the therapist will help the client build skill in noticing their arousal patterns, and noticing how their need for space changes at different moments. This will depend on skills from Key One, including the body as a gauge (0 to 10), noticing whether sensations feel comfortable or not, tracking ripples of arousal even when they are well within the window of tolerance. Once the client is having some success at noticing, invite them to signal you to pause *when they feel any shift in arousal or somatic activation*—in other words, they feel like you are at a boundary. This is congruence: when the body says "close enough" natural physical signals emerge to signal the partner.

The next step is to support the client to explore with a horse in a safe enclosure where the horse can be at liberty. Support the client to practice different approaches, observing somatic and behavioral signals in self and horse. The goal is naturalness and confidence, and a balanced awareness of self and other. The work should quickly catch hold and express itself as an increased bodily poise in the client, with the horses showing more care and attentiveness in the client's presence.

The fluid language of space is very powerful in the horse herd. I like to acquaint clients with elements of this spatial language. For instance a respectful horse will stretch its neck to reach across the distance of a person's space bubble, offering what I call "a meet and greet." This is not the same as "meet and cuddle"—

although when touch is invited, the client can be encouraged to identify boundaries in sensitive areas of the horse such as the face, ears, groin and flanks. Sometimes the horse simply prefers the "hang out zone," happy to have the person's company as long as no touch demands are made—no pressure. There are also times where the horse may be so eager to connect that it feels a bit intrusive, offering the perfect opportunity to teach a foundational boundaries move: "one step back."

Photo 1. *"Rock back and sigh" = wait and lower arousal. HEAL student Rebecca Lobb*

Photo 2. *"One step back, please." Leigh with student Jan Stewart in The Horse-Human Connection workshop. Photos used with permission.*

With young clients, clients who are very concrete thinkers or clients who might become dissociative, it may be helpful to have the horse on the lead line. The halter and rope represent structure and support for both boundaries and connection, not a way to force control on the horse. In other words the halter and rope are there as an aid to understanding and to finding the right distance for performing various activities. For instance, running beside the horse as it trots requires a bigger space cushion than walking beside the horse. When there is a bond of attention and engagement between client and horse, this can be performed without any tension being put on the rope.

Numerous activities—actually, almost all activities—at liberty and on the lead line, as well as riding activities, are rich with opportunities to explore and articulate boundaries. Moving with the horse as described above transforms the dance of boundaries and permission by enabling alignment and mirroring, which happen naturally as the human and horse interact from a safe distance.

✤ EFPL HORSE ACTIVITY ✤
Boundary Sensing and Setting

This exercise helps to increase personal boundary awareness, and prepares the client for boundary practice with the horses. It is an experience that will be new for many practitioners of EFPL. It takes practice and experience for the clinician to master the intricacies of this human-to-human exercise, as well as the boundary exercises and interactions with the horses.

Procedure for human-to-human exercise:

1. Take the client outside. Moving from the office to the outdoors—any change in location—is an opportunity to explore fluctuations (what I call 'ripples') in their arousal level, valence and texture. Find an open area and stand far enough apart that both you and the client feel certain that you are not in each other's "energy field." This distance is often 12 to 15 feet, or more. Assess the client's and your own current baseline arousal.

2. In a typical scenario I let the client know I am going to approach at a steady natural pace. I always make sure to say explicitly that I will not do anything to startle or surprise them. They are to carefully monitor their arousal sensations and any body movements that they become aware of.

3. I begin my approach, careful to regulate my own energy. My eyes are upon them but with what horsemen call "soft eyes." Some clients have transparent reactions, others are harder to read, but this first approach reliably produces noticeable subjective arousal in most people. A smaller percentage may experience drops in their arousal and usually at first this person insists that they feel no change. It may be helpful with some adult clients—and youth too—to teach them to monitor their carotid pulse in the neck in order to have objective data. WITH A STEADY APPROACH THE BODY WILL EVIDENCE INVOLUNTARY REACTIONS TO THE IMPENDING PROXIMITY.

4. Involuntary reactions to proximity include eye blinking, smiling, jaw tightening, hand movement, rocking back, subtle posture changes, tightening of stomach, chest or throat, or frozen facial muscles. The brain searches for the reassurance of social signals. Exploring the wealth of reactions opens up new levels of self knowing for most clients. Exchange roles, allowing the client to approach you, trying to sense your subtle boundaries. *Remember that the client needs this awareness of the tiniest cues of interest/arousal because very soon their partner in this exercise will be the horse!*

5. An important part of this exercise is to instruct the client to signal you, as you approach, to build in some pauses during your approach. This is the 'rock back and sigh' maneuver. In this instance, I will again approach the client—but this time when the client notices arousal changes, he or she will signal by holding up a hand. This is where I take one or more steps back, relax my abdomen and let my breath out. When the clients arousal has returned to baseline, they will signal me "come on" with a wave of their hand.

6. Some of the important principles that I use in processing are: finding the right distance for this moment so that both partners feel relaxed; matching strength with strength when setting a boundary; being precise and saying thank you when the horse rewards with precision. All kinds of things can go slightly wrong so that the boundary is a little muddy and misunderstandings can occur. The therapist will assist the client in finding grace with the boundary dance with their equine partner.

7. Boundary work with the horse can and should be done in all kinds of situations because boundaries are quite contextual in any relationship. If the client is with a horse at liberty there are three concepts to explain: the intention to meet and greet (including the body language); boundaries regarding touch (face more sensitive than shoulder); and how to find the "hangout zone" of both the person and the horse. A hangout zone has both parties connected by a comfortable space, making no demands on each other.

8. Clients should be familiarized with boundary tools, such as a whip, wand or "stick and string", and their gentle yet effective use. Help your client discover how to negotiate boundaries that are connective while maintaining individuality and autonomous space.

Photo 3. Equine Greeting Ritual. *Frieda and Galant, who had a close and enduring love for each other, share a meet and greet on a frosty morning.*

✺ EFPL HORSE ACTIVITY ✺
Signs of Unhealthy Boundaries in the Round Pen

In every session your EFPL clients will have opportunities to explore the nuances of boundaries with the horses. In one session a client might approach the horse or horses at liberty in a field for a 'meet and greet,' in another the task might be to capture the horse's attention by 'knocking on the door' or to befriend the horse by honoring his 'hang out zone.' Help the client understand that it's OK to get it 'wrong,' that the relationship with the horse is durable and forgiving.

Here are signs of unhealthy boundary patterns and unconscious signals that almost always indicate a level of unresolved history and possible dissociation.

- Generally poor body proprioception, and poor awareness of the space bubble. Slow down any action or agenda in the horse activity, and assist the client in staying present or grounded. Return to a safe zone and easier activities with the horse until the participant regains equilibrium.
- Failing to maintain appropriate space cushions can also have implications for the relationship. Only a dominant horse would crowd another toward the rail of an arena and when a human allows such behavior the horse will assume dominance.
- Working too close to the horse, reluctance to use stick or whip when necessary to maintain safe distance, or pushing touch or attention at a horse who is not inviting it—all of these indicate patterns of unhealthy boundaries in the horse arena.

Healthy, permeable boundaries allow the exchange of information, such as signals sent by the horse, which are critical to successful connecting. The goal is to assist the participant in accurate reading of the horse's boundary signals. Falling in love with the horse, allowing a horse with questionable intentions into personal space, or disregarding boundaries to be nice to the horse are all boundary "red flags."

Here are some common mistakes that we all can make with humans as well as horses: Not noticing when the horse invades your boundaries. Accepting touch that you don't want. Believing the horse knows or can anticipate your needs. Not asking for help when you really want it. Not being sure of your own boundaries until you notice a feeling of violation.

EFPL FACILITATION TOPIC
Negotiating Boundaries, with Love

Boundaries protect our love for one another by protecting our physical, emotional, intellectual, spiritual, space, as well as theirs, i.e., those with whom we interact.

Horses speak the primary languages of space, timing, touch, body language, feeling (limbic mammalian brain), intent, and congruence and-or incongruence with human mammals.

Skin is an essential boundary to the body, and is a good metaphor for the other boundaries: a semi-permeable membrane that absorbs nutrients yet protects from intrusions or toxicity.

Good Boundary Practices	**Poor Boundary Practices**
Use boundaries to take care of yourself	Boundaries used to manipulate/control/punish
Limits are chosen by you: verbal and non-verbal	Either/or: wall building or no boundaries
Negotiated with integrity, clarity &confidence	Fear of loss prevents boundary building (abandonment fears)
Responsible; safe; balanced	
Sensitive to feelings (limbic connectedness)	Give too much/take too much
Trustworthy; reasonable, natural and logical	Too sensitive/not sensitive enough
Consistent in awareness/communication	Mixed messages
Congruent (avoid mixed messages)	Inconsistent in awareness/communication
Sensitive to the arousal of those we interact with and love	Incongruent/not trustworthy
	Not feeling or seeing the other's arousal
Enforceable: May be rigid if threatened with abuse	No follow through on consequences

Mutual respect and understanding are the goals of boundary maintenance. Tend your boundaries with care, like a beloved garden. Think and feel "on your feet" in the moment.

KEY TWO Vignette
Tina in PTSD group session one and two

In the first session of our PTSD group, we educated the group of adolescent girls about Key One, and the importance of tuning in to their own senses and feelings, for safety with the horses. Tina's level of anxious arousal was obviously outside of her 'window of tolerance.' While the other girls participated in the group discussion and got to know each other on breaks, Tina curled into herself, arms crossed around her middle. Tina wouldn't speak to us and ignored our directives for group activities. Our team's attempts to engage her only made her sullen. I wondered that first day if Tina would be able to keep up with the group when the horse activities became more complex.

After the classroom activity, participants went out to "meet the herd"—assigned with tracking their subjective "activation" level (activation with either positive or negative responsive feelings) as they met six horses (separated in individual paddocks). When the girls met the horses from across a fence (no touching, yet), it was apparent that Beau was drawn to Tina. Tina did not move on to meet other horses, but stood frozen as if soaking up Beau's penetrating gaze (Beau ignored every girl but Tina). The emotional resonance was palpable. Tina denied feeling anything, but when the other girls gently teased her: He *liked* you! Tina suppressed a slight smile and determinedly kept her eyes downward. I considered this mutual attraction (resonance) as I planned to pair each girl with a horse. Beau is our most rambunctious horse, and Tina the most fragile client in this group, nonetheless I decided to trust the horse and I paired Beau with Tina for the remaining weeks of group sessions.

In the second session, the arena was full with five inexperienced (and affectively labile) girls handling horses on lead lines. A few of the girls would simply merge with the horse if they could; conversely one girl was very afraid. Tina, however, was apathetic, withdrawn. We focused on Key Two, Boundaries. Team member David kept a watchful eye on Tina and Beau. Beau has a habit of playful head-rubbing, and right off the bat he almost knocked Tina off her feet with a turn of his head. David showed Tina how to "block"—when Beau gave a sideways glance Tina learned to hold her hand up in the signal that says, "watch out for me." Tina had to watch Beau, too, in order to be timely with her signal. Soon Tina and Beau were communicating, and he settled beside her. Over and over girl and horse practiced this simple boundary interaction, as if it were ultimately absorbing for both of them.

Such a simple move, but between Tina and Beau a palpable bond was forming. But would it be enough to help Tina succeed with her peers?

More about Tina in Chapter 6 …

MORE ABOUT KEY TWO: BOUNDARIES

Keeping somebody at "arm's length" isn't just a metaphor for maintaining a personal boundary, it is a scientific fact governing space. The invisible bubble around the body—approximately the length and width of your arm—is called peripersonal space by neuroscientists (Blakeslee and Blakeslee, 2007, chap. 7). The brain effectively rents this space as you walk around, extending and shrinking your world in fluid and infinitely creative ways.

How you sense and react to the space around your own body, as well as the personal space of others, is the result of the body's supreme map-making abilities. It is literally mapping peripersonal space, moment by moment, to enable you to navigate life virtually unaware. You may "grow" to include the interior of your car, the length of a gardening tool, or the 1,000 pounds of horse under your saddle. A child or lover may be incorporated into the body's personal bubble of space and effectively become part of you, as far as the brain is concerned. This is also how you are able to feel things apart from actually touching them—the surface of the road under car tires or the difference in texture between butter or a steak at the end of your knife.

When you learn something new or navigate an unfamiliar space—the back of a strange horse, a new apartment—your mind and body immediately get busy molding and assimilating the new space into maps your physical body can use. Outstanding athletes have superior body "mandalas" (a metaphor for the physical network of body maps located deep inside your brain) related to athletic games and the objects and spaces represented by them (Blakeslee & Blakeslee, 2007). Their bodies instinctively know how to play the game based on a network of subconscious and invisible maps—a somatic GPS. In equestrian sports, the horse and rider are sharing personal space and body mandalas as they navigate a difficult obstacle.

Horse and rider can be a beautiful example of harmony within shared personal space. Even in the quiet dynamics of approach, retreat, grooming and leading, clients at HEAL begin to develop a sense of their personal space as rightfully their own, a tool of their selfhood and expression. It's wonderful to see clients develop confidence—even joy—as they begin to own their space and therefore more fully inhabit the body it contains.

The brain actually contains cells to track what happens within the peripersonal space. When something penetrates this space those cells begin firing (Blakeslee and Blakeslee, 2007 p. 117). This space can also be violated. The person "in your face" is not only confrontational in words, they are assaulting the peripersonal space. What happens within physical boundaries—the sensitive highly tuned peripersonal space—dramatically affects one's sense of self.

Besides mapping the physical body, the brain is busy constructing the body "schema" or the body's felt experience per sensations from the skin, muscles, etc. It is mostly unconscious and goes on moment by moment, situation by situation. Without these amazing, unseen cartographers you would not even realize you had a body! The body mandala and schema work together—informing each other as new skills are acquired as well as referencing expectations—what you think is likely to happen—and ingrained beliefs (Blakeslee and Blakeslee, 2007 p. 39). A disconnect can occur when body image is added into the mix.

Body image is how you consciously feel about your body and ingrained beliefs about it. These are birthed in childhood and begin to set a pattern by adolescence. Body image beliefs are influenced from many sources including the family of origin, and religious and cultural sources. They are often smothered in shame and self-hatred. Beliefs you hold—or, more appropriately, that hold you—may not be visible, but they are stored and organized in your brain and are just as real as its cellular make-up. How do we know? Your held beliefs are stored in brain circuits that fire in response to predictions and expectations about the world around you based on past experiences. Perceptions are often not reality.

Besides its starring role in the sense of touch, the body's barrier of skin is a good metaphor for the need and proper use of personal boundaries. The skin is the largest organ in the body. It is porous, flexible, sensitive, receptive, and *protective*. It is constantly sensing the environment, preventing contaminants from reaching and damaging fragile internal organs, disposing of waste, and welcoming nourishment in the way of food, oxygen, and water. The skin senses and responds to the environment, moment by moment, and transmits the messages it receives to critical body systems. It can be damaged and wounded, but it heals quickly and reestablishes an environment of protection.

Chapter Five

The Third Key: Mending the Divided Self

*"The critical inner voice exists to varying degrees in every person ...
it keeps us locked inside our defense systems, while our healthier side
strives for freedom from the constraints of these defenses."*

Firestone, Firestone, and Catlett
Conquer Your Critical Inner Voices

THERAPEUTIC STRATEGY IN KEY THREE: MENDING THE DIVIDED SELF

Regarding the so-called "tri-brain," Lewis et al. (2001, p. 31) remind us that, "Evolution's stuttering process has fashioned a brain that is fragmented and inharmonious, and to some degree composed of players of competing interests." It is helpful to remember that the triune brain is a hierarchical system, with survival coming before logic, and the short term often taking precedence over long term. In the presence of mild to severe levels of threat, a cascade of defensive reactions occurs, occurring in three general categories: social engagement or appealing to others, mobilizing defenses of fight or flight, and immobilizing defenses of freezing or feigned death (Ogden et al., 2006, p. 89).

Not just real threat, but the presence of implicit *threat cues or reminders* can activate defenses, which are often out of proportion to a realistic assessment of actual threat. How could it be otherwise, since a bottom-up process commandeers feeling and thinking processes from the brainstem up. Often called "triggers," some can be explosive "hot buttons," some are avoidant "cold buttons."

With horses and with people, survival depends on being attached to a herd. Under conditions of moderate threat (or perceived threat), defensive reactions activate the autonomic responses called the "social engagement system"—expressions and behaviors to elicit connection, help and support from others. This may include appealing, persuading, posturing, and appeasing behaviors. Sufficiently severe threat conditions trigger the 'fight or flight' mobilizing defenses that activate the body; or even the immobilizing defenses that result in motionlessness or collapse. Under these conditions, the 'roads' (i.e., neural pathways) leading to the 'land of logic' (thinking neocortex) are temporarily closed.

Using Key Three the therapist supports the client in their ability to manage arousal by using and accepting regulation in order to work on more highly charged issues within the window of tolerance. I constantly emphasize this to HEAL clients: learn to *soothe, not stuff* your feelings. Soothing is healthy; it enables listening to feelings. Stuffing and suppressing emotion is not healthy or functional—and any horse will tell you the same.

In young mammals, potential abandonment quickly elicits distress vocalizations and frantic attempts to signal caregivers. This is social anxiety, also called separation anxiety and referred to in neuroscience as the PANIC circuit. Like RAGE (which frequently overlaps), social PANIC (and the incongruent behavior that results) is a leading cause of destructive negative arousal and serious pathological behaviors.

The horses themselves can provide dramatic examples of separation distress. When this happens during EFPL it can be an opportunity to learn about this brain circuit that signals alarm when attachments feel threatened. A horse that is perfectly calm with herdmates can become extremely distressed when taken away from the others, and will frantically pace and call loudly. If not properly managed, horses can seriously injure themselves by their frantic attempts to rejoin the herd. Social mammals carry the potential for separation panic at all times; solitary confinement is torture that can lead to madness.

The PANIC system primes an individual for frantic attempts to avoid abandonment, desperate attempts to reconnect, and the fear of annihilation or being cast out of the herd. A subtle impression that the love object might abandon or disregard, can swiftly cause a PANIC reaction in the amygdale, effectively shutting off rational thought.

The effects of the resulting "divided self" range from constant self-criticism, to inability to successfully meet the challenges of life and relationships, to a fractured experience of dissociation or psychosis when trauma memories become "hot buttons." The divided self has many faces, all of which involve defending ourselves against something we don't want to feel or experience in ourselves. In short, the divided self can encompass many types and intensities of psychological defense. Defenses always produce either heightened arousal or numbing avoidance, which escalate rapidly according to the client's subjective perception of threat.

Horses will clearly sense this heightened energy of threat or defense. With EFPL we have the opportunity to create mild limbic anxiety in the here-and-now, along with lots of support for soothing and revision.

With this key, the therapist can help the client explore specific social anxieties and attachment patterns that prompt excessive reactivity, inappropriate to the present situation. Excessive reactivity can inhibit behavior which warrants expression (for example, it can cause a person to not set a needed boundary). By the phrase "Divided Self," I mean to identify incongruence, rigid defenses and belief systems, which kick in to replace our more thoughtful intentions. I want to help clients become aware of such "divided self" experiences.

The ANS gives each individual a unique and variable resiliency that includes both temperament and life experience, a resiliency that is needed for emotional and situational stressors in the present. This is the body's stress tolerance "window." Stress tolerance impacts our ability to function effectively and think clearly in the moment; over the long term it impacts our health and well-being. The body gauge described by the 0-10 arousal scale (in Chapter Three) points to a 'window of tolerance' that defines our ability to think and function well, even in upsetting circumstances.

A combination of cognitive with previously taught somatic strategies are helpful to strengthen self-soothing capacity, to help the client become comfortable with the vulnerability that mature, authentic relationships entail. It is important to emphasize the client's growing capacity to *soothe, not stuff* their feelings. It is OK for a client to feel deep feelings, strong feelings, or to feel upset with important others. Expanding the window of tolerance for emotions is an important goal of therapy.

Practicing healthy ways of managing arousal enables the process of rewriting the neural pathways for emotion in the brain. Compared to the superhighways of trauma-conditioned reactions and behavior, these healthier (but unused) neural pathways have the fragility of faint deer trails in the wilderness. While first traveling them the client will feel vulnerable and exposed. For those who have been wounded within human relationships, practice with a horse may be the best—and safest—way to begin a difficult process. "Working with horses … un-teaches an old pattern of not trusting ourselves in relationships," (Lavender, 2006, p. 45).

As therapy progresses the client becomes more capable of tolerating strong emotion in order to work effectively with it. It permits a more complete exploration of somatic awareness as the client navigates more ambiguous situations (for instance, the open-ended reflective sessions described in this chapter). The horses generally have a strong soothing and grounding effect on clients, their silent responsiveness helping the client to articulate desires and anxieties. The responsive actions of the horse may be mundane, or quite novel—often helping to activate the deep inner world of the client.

The therapist and client will also explore Key Three as the "divided self" gets revealed during moderate challenges, such as enforcing a "no-eating boundary" when the horse is standing in lush grass, or navigating a situation where the horse refuses a request . As the client attempts such tasks, it is easy to identify self-narrative that is self-deprecating, overly intellectual, or self-justifying. The horse can always sense the lack of inner certainty. The divided self results in not being able to make a connection with the horse in the here and now because defenses have been engaged. Such indications of a divided self will tell you exactly how the client similarly blocks feeling-based relationships with humans.

TYPICAL EFPL ACTIVITIES FOR KEY THREE

The growing relationship with the horse provides many good opportunities for the client to identify their own areas of reactivity or inhibition. Open-ended, non-agenda reflective sessions can be very powerful. The person is invited to be with the horse at liberty in a fairly large pen or arena. By tracking their own feeling states and cognitions and also maintaining awareness of the horse, the client can find a wholeness of relating where abstract fears of not being good enough do not seem to belong. The challenge, and the gift, lies in the emotional vulnerability of unknown outcome and no agenda. Reflective sessions allow the client to form a new relationship with vulnerability.

Reflective sessions are most powerful when the client is in an affectively potent state, what I call "full of feeling." However, I do not mean full of sentiment; literally I mean that the client is in touch with somatic markers that are energized. Reflective sessions will be further amplified if you allow a process of mutual choosing between horse and client. When the client is in an affectively potent state, and a particular horse is visibly moved to work with that client, truly amazing things often happen that are limbically powerful. Quite commonly, the client has a strong desire to be affirmed or wanted by the horse—but the horse shows little response. The client is confronted with their own doubts: he doesn't like me, I look stupid, etc. This is arousal. When the client is able to soothe, the abdomen relaxes and the breath comes easier. Almost always the horse will approach when the client is able to feel their need without acting it out.

Reflective sessions can be conducted in a variety of ways. If the horse has grass to graze on it can alter their response to the client—especially if they've not had time to get their hunger sated. Clients who have achieved safety and competence with boundaries may at times go out with the herd in the pasture for self reflection and inspiration from the horses. This gives a very powerful impression of the web of energy that holds the herd together, an inherent sense of belonging while still having individual freedoms.

For the client who might not be ready for such an unstructured experience, I often use something very simple, such as bringing the horse out on fresh ungrazed grass with the instruction to hold the boundary that the horse is not to eat. Not simply to keep the horse's head up, but to communicate the boundary so that the horse will relax and the client has a minimum of reminding to maintain. Such simple exercises often stimulate social anxiety, and reveal the client's evasions (or nagging).

Clients who find it difficult to tolerate vulnerability will tend toward the reactive side. In this case it is often better to provide more structure by offering a small but concrete challenge. For example, I like to have clients walk the horse on the lead line from the arena down to the end of the driveway, where the horse will tend to become distracted by his own separation anxiety, unless the client can provide sufficient regulation and safety. This allows the client to act, but in a thoughtful vein.

✢ EFPL FACILITATION TOPIC ✢
The Body as Resource (Body Scan)*

The body scan is a more advanced procedure than simply tracking arousal and sensations. The client is encouraged to enter into an imaginative dialogue with their own body sensations and awareness, including subtle impressions or "intuitions" having to do with others or the environment. The full body scan is an appropriate deepening for clients who are able to tolerate and regulate feelings while tracking arousal and describing sensations.

To engage the body's innate wisdom effectively takes practice. Over time, with practice, the physical body becomes the safe place it was meant to be. Overwhelming feelings of fear, panic or rage have their source in unresolved history. The clinician must be ready to assist the client in regulating difficult feelings that threaten to exceed the window of tolerance.

With trauma, the tolerance for awareness of bodily sensations and primary emotions narrows in order to survive. Being accompanied and regulated by a caring and trusting person, and/or the horse, is often the initial key to widening the window of tolerance. "Feeling felt" (Siegel, 2010, p. 10) helps the client connect back to self and regulate their internal state. Limbic resonance and limbic regulation with a safe person and/or horse can help a person to feel safe enough to feel their own feelings. The goal is to help the client contain and experience feelings, gradually expanding the window of tolerance.

Procedures:

1. *Map the sensations.* In a neutral environment, teach the client to scan the body in a systematic fashion, focusing attention briefly on each main part. Notice arousal and associated sensations; also be open to subjective sensations such as colors or images. Notice the sensations without trying to change them or "relax out of them."

2. For the sensations that stand out, support the client to *dialog with their body* by expanding the sensation and asking it for the information it may be holding. (So-called "negative" as well as "positive" sensations can hold valuable information.) They can imagine breathing into the sensation, sending it oxygen and awareness. This can be visualized as the sensation "speaking," or "sending a message " to the mind, in the

---
* Thanks to Kathleen Barry Ingram, MA for her contributions to this section.

form of an image, a brief "text message," a color, a memory, etc.

3. Help the client to *assess the result*. When they receive a message or a clue, whether it makes "logical sense" or not, have them check back in with the sensation. If it has released, this means the message was received to your body's satisfaction. (Proceed to step 4.) If the sensation has intensified, ask your body if there is another message. If the sensation stays the same, give your body some time and check in with it later.

Clinician beware! The client may receive a message very different from the one you think they should or would expect based on your training.

4. *Encourage the client to get a new baseline reading frequently* and continually dialogue with their body, especially when entering a new or stressful situation. Assist the client to stay in contact with their body and notice changes. Body awareness is not an emotion, rather a combination of distinct and often subtle body sensations.

The sensing body becomes an internal compass for negotiating boundaries, navigating emotions and engaging with others, while maintaining a secure sense of self. It is the hub of mindfulness. Working with clients and using the body scan along with the 0–10 scale of arousal begins a dialogue for them to continue to use on a daily basis.

✢ EFPL HORSE ACTIVITY ✢
Individual Reflective Session (for Adult Client)*

Reflective sessions develop a client's ability to allow connection and support to happen, rather than trying so hard to make them happen. The reflective experience increases the client's comfort with vulnerability, and often gently reveals the client's blocks to connection and intimacy. Reflective sessions assist clients in the skill of tracking internal process and noticing the horse's response to their internal states; they have opportunities to respond to the horse's overtures or initiate their own. Many clients will face the challenge of "just being."

Reflective sessions are deceptively simple to set up—the art is in the facilitation. When the client is in authentic contact with feelings, you will find the horses to be the most limbically responsive, which can cause them to make quite remarkable gestures and behavior or expressions. Lying down near the person, running circles around them, nuzzling into their heart chakra—I have observed these and many other unique and limbically purposeful actions, even in horses that are in EFPL for the first time.

Horses respond to people who are full of feeling, but this does not include misplaced sentiment or the demands of enmeshment. It is important for the clinician to have a good feel for the degree of accompaniment each client desires or requires. In general, for reflective sessions, less guidance from the therapist allows the horse to come forward in the horse's own time and way.

---

* Thanks to Kathleen Barry Ingram, MA for her contributions to this section.

Preparations:

The client should be acquainted with safety instruction and boundary setting from previous EFPL sessions. Similarly, the clinician's understanding of the client's capacity and patterns for emotional regulation should be developing through the sessions that have already occurred. Have the client choose a horse through a feeling-based process that allows client and therapist to notice emotional resonance with particular horses. Then take a short break while the horse is led to the round pen, small paddock or arena. Pasture can complicate the session, because of course the horse will often graze—this doesn't always prevent them from connecting or communicating (depending on how hungry they are), but can make their language harder for humans to spot. The chosen spot should be equipped with a stool in case the client wishes to sit, and a boundary tool such as a carrot stick or short whip (even if you think it's unlikely to be needed).

Procedures for the clinician:

1. Begin with the client outside the pen, with the client facing away from the horse, who is in the pen. Guide, or support the client in a full-body self-awareness body scan. The client is invited to share and process the most prominent sensations. (See previous EFPL Practice Technique: Body as Resource.)

2. Have the client turn around and face the horse, and describe any changes or new sensations they are feeling in their body. In the majority of cases, the client will feel the calming, affirming sensations of regulation from the horse. The client may feel "a message" from the horse or a strong connection through the heart field. Note: If the client feels increased anxious arousal at this point, proceed with some caution, allowing the client to work with the horse from outside the pen first. Very rarely, the horse can become agitated prior to the person entering the pen; usually this reflects a limbic intention to connect with the person, but still warrants caution.

3. The pre-session body scan and processing often reveal a natural focus for the reflective session. It can be helpful to ask the client to tune in to their heart or center, and articulate any desire or wish for today's time with the horse. For example:

    > *"Let's see if the horse has any suggestions. Breathe into your heart and feel your awareness beating outward through your heart field and touching the horse's heart field. Ask the horse, "Do you have any information for me, or any suggestions for how I might realize my heart's desire (or truest intention) with you today?"*

4. Open the gate for the client while reminding them it is OK to ask you for help or suggestions at any time. You may also remind the person of some safety considerations, such as not getting between the horse and the fence.

5. Let the client experiment for several minutes. If the person seems stuck, go ahead and gently offer some reflection and help by asking, *"What are you experiencing?"* Resist becoming instructive; follow the client's experience and what you think the horse may be experiencing or trying to say.

∽ EFPL FACILITATION TOPIC ∾
The Limbic Questions for EFPL Facilitation

The limbic system looks for safety, belonging and control in relationships. In new relationships the limbic brain is stimulated to test and figure out the dynamics of unfolding connection. These are questions the horse will be asking of the human client. The questions point to the needs for TRUST and relationship STRUCTURE in order for the brainstem and limbic system to be adequately regulated. Breaks in the limbic connection—even seemingly small ruptures—will erode the vibrancy of the bond between the horse and the person. In EFPL these small ruptures offer huge opportunities for examining unresolved history. You will find fruitful "threads" for facilitation by exploring these questions.

What am I most afraid of? What do I need most from you?

Will you ask my permission? (Respect me/my boundaries?)

What are you asking of me? Do you notice me and my language?

What am I asking of you? Do you understand what I am saying?

Can I count on you? How consistent are you?

Do you mean what you say? Do your actions match up with your words?

What am I feeling now? (arousal, sensations) What's my partner feeling?

Are you kind? Are you present? Do you see my feelings?

Are you for me/against me? Are you doing this *to* me or *with* me?

Am I safe/are you safe? Who is 'over' whom?

Who do I need to look out for and why?

What emotions am I most reluctant to experience in myself or coming from others? How do I protect myself? At what point do I withdraw?

When the connection is damaged, do we attempt to repair? Forgive injuries?

❦ KEY THREE Vignette ❦
Linda—Middle Stage of individual EFPL

Remember Linda, whose feelings were locked inside with her breath? By her work over many sessions Linda is gaining a sense of security in her own body and an ability to work with boundaries so they help her communicate clearly to the horse. Now entering the middle stage of therapy, I want Linda to experience a reflective session—time spent with the horse at liberty, with no explicit agenda. An equine partner is chosen by a felt resonance. Cloud's interest in Linda made her feel in the moment "like he's calling to me." In a reflective session the client relies on feeling-based processes, which make up the feedback loop between the human and the horse. There is no outcome to strive for, just an opportunity for the client to be with their own feelings, in the presence of an equine "therapist." Remarkable things can happen in this vulnerable space of possibility.

Linda was now better able to sense her body and gauge feelings. It was important to proceed carefully as I guided Linda in a self-awareness body scan. Previously unexamined memories and sensory impressions had already surfaced at times, causing Linda to be almost overwhelmed by anxiety or self-hatred. We had recently begun working on identifying such triggers to a false self.

During the body scan, Linda was able to soothe some sensations, such as the "butterflies" she identified as "fear of rejection." Most prominent was a heavy, dark, sad affect in her solar plexus. This, she said, is her fear that a successful intimate relationship will never happen for her, because she is "so damaged." By carefully tracking arousal, Linda becomes aware that these interpretations are not productive. She is able to stay with the feeling itself. Tears fall.

When Linda turns to face Cloud, he is standing quietly in the pen, watching her. Linda feels a distinct calming. She enters the pen but Cloud does not approach her; he walks the perimeter. He stops at a pile of manure, and spends a long time sniffing, very absorbed. He raises his head proudly, nostrils wide as he tests the air, then paws the ground. At first Linda keeps her distance, fascinated by his purposeful behavior but also cautious. She tentatively approaches, and he turns his head, touching her solar plexus. Together they face into the wind. Afterward Linda says, "I felt acceptance ... and protected." Cloud was acting out the limbic role of herd stallion, and he is the most dominant male in our herd. Cloud can be quite fierce as a protector of our small herd at HEAL.

Linda's vivid and memorable impressions represent her new pathways, worthy of cultivation:

I AM WORTH PROTECTING. MALES CAN BE STRONG AND GENTLE.

More about Linda in Chapter 7 …

MORE ABOUT KEY THREE: MENDING THE DIVIDED SELF

The ability of the amygdale to prompt immediate action without cognitive process was termed an "*amygdale hijack*" by Daniel Goleman in his 1996 book *Emotional Intelligence*. Goleman uses the term to describe emotional responses from people, which are out of measure with the actual circumstance, because a much more emotional (but usually unrealistic) threat has been triggered. Says Goleman, "The hijacking occurs in an instant, triggering this reaction crucial moments before the neocortex, the thinking brain, has had a chance to glimpse fully what is happening, let alone decide if it is a good idea" (1996, p. 14). An amygdale hijack exhibits three signs: strong emotional reaction, sudden onset, and post-episode realization that the reaction was inappropriate.

Negative arousal is heightened arousal stemming from the primitive activations of FEAR, RAGE, and PANIC. The heightened arousal has a dramatic, measurable, impact on the Sympathetic Nervous System (SNS) of our body's ANS, which controls our core Heart-Breathing-Mind control center. Affective arousal originating in the brainstem and limbic system processes information milliseconds faster than the rational mind (Reivich and Schatte, 2002)—which is effectively "cut off" from responding. Highly aroused negative emotion triggers intense feelings and (sometimes) impulsive actions (Siegel, 1999).

Psychologists agree that stress arises from both positive and negative events. A much anticipated wedding may be as stressful as the loss of a job. Positive arousal includes excitement, anticipation or hopefulness. Negative arousal is rage, desperation, terror, anxiety/panic, fear, and trauma. The most extreme is traumatic stress. Thinking and behavior become disrupted when arousal moves beyond the boundaries of the window of tolerance. This window may be quite narrow, especially in cases of PTSD, because the window of tolerance is directly influenced by experiential history (Siegel, 1999, p. 254).

Arousal that is outside of the window of tolerance may be unregulated, or may become *dysregulated* (a snowballing effect). Heightened arousal causes a very narrow mental focus. In fact, it can effectively "shut down" the roadways from the limbic system to cortex, causing a person (or a horse) to lose focus on what she or he really wants (Fruzetti, 2006). Increased reactivity to social stress increases arousal to an even higher level. All of this explains why a client's most troublesome symptoms are not accessible to the rational mind. In EFPL we have the chance to explore troublesome patterns experientially.

Escape includes withdrawal and dissociation, which may be obvious only through non-verbal signals (Fruzzetti, 2006, p. 3). Once the orientation is on escape, the person is in a primitive activation state of FEAR. Sometimes a contributor to relationship failure is an attitude of "go along to get along," which can be based in a deep-seated avoidance of negotiation or conflict, an escape orientation.

The clinician must be an astute observer of ANS body changes, and coach the client to do the same for themselves. Particularly noticeable to the client will be their respiration, heart rate, muscle tension in jaws, face or elsewhere, sweating or loss of appetite. The clinician is most likely to notice visible signs such as posture, facial expression, flushing, or dilated pupils. In very strong reactions, the autonomic system may slump into a pattern of passive dissociation. The client in this case will lose tone and become pallid and less responsive.

Is some negative arousal OK? Yes. Some negative arousal, when the person is still able to think clearly, gives an important signal: keep that arousal from getting higher. The therapist should help the client start recovery by converting that negative energy toward positive energy. The client needs some arousal to stay in the game, without exceeding the window of optimum arousal.

"Recovery means decreasing the disorganizing effects of a particular episode of arousal," according to Siegel (1999, p. 258). The goal is to move back within the boundaries of the "window of tolerance," helping the client to "push the envelope" but not break it. A flood of emotions without an effective recovery process will result in prolonged states of disorganization that are ineffective and potentially harmful.

Strategy for client to recover from destructive negative arousal:
1. Notice arousal level while it is low and before thinking is impaired.
2. Know how to reduce emotional arousal level, using breath and thought anchors.
3. Breathe slowly, deeply, to get your ANS in balance, which will bring down arousal.
4. Before reacting, take the space and time needed to restore equilibrium.
5. If you need time to process what is happening, ask for that time.
6. Carefully and clearly consider your boundaries.
7. When your arousal level is down and you can clearly recall what you really want, then you are ready to use effective communication skills to resolve a problem.
8. Recovery strategy can be effectively practiced unilaterally, with positive results!

Not only is it painful to have negative emotional arousal be high for a long time, it also means that during this time, individuals are vulnerable to both increased reactivity and to becoming dysregulated, because their arousal is already elevated. High emotion sensitivity, high reactivity and slow return to equilibrium create vulnerability to becoming dysregulated in a variety of situations (Fruzetti, 2006; Linehan, 1993). Prolonged high negative arousal exerts a significant stress load on the body, which can be cumulative over time.

Cognitivists like Aaron Beck discovered that beliefs and rumination can add to and even cause anxiety, not just be symptomatic of it. Certainly, arousal tends to snowball as somatic and cerebral processes play upon each other (Reivich and Schatte, 2002). The central feature of anxiety is thought (belief), a top down process. On the other hand, bottom up feelings of anxiety can convince us that we're completely ill-prepared to handle the adversities in life. If we begin to take control where we can, anxiety will recede.

Clients should be taught the cognitive model for soothing negative arousal and working with their thoughts. We want clients to actively seek and build self-narratives that emphasize confidence and competence. Using the cognitive model helps the client "train" their cortex to be more helpful, even when arousal is high. Since anxiety and fear affect almost every system in the body, the "calming" step must be completed before proceeding to solutions.

1. Stop what-if, catastrophic thinking.
2. Deal specifically with real problems. Define what is known and unknown.
3. Estimate the probabilities of your worst-case fears.
4. Generate best-case alternatives to broaden your perception.
5. What are the most likely implications?

Daily practice is essential and doubly essential for success in relationships. More practice, leads to more resilience. *The goal: manageable anxiety.*

Chapter Six

The Fourth Key: Play of Yin and Yang

"Play systems help generate a diversity of emotional behaviors upon which learning can operate ... Play circuitry allows other emotional operating systems, especially social ones, to be exercised in the relative safety of one's home environment."

Jaak Panksepp

Affective Neuroscience: The Foundations of Human and Animal Emotions

THERAPEUTIC STRATEGY IN KEY FOUR: THE PLAY OF YIN AND YANG

The ancient philosophy of Taoism describes the natural harmony of two complementary principles: Yin is negative, dark, receptive and feminine; Yang is positive, bright, active and masculine. The interaction of these principles is thought to maintain the harmony of the universe and everything within it. Every human being has a capacity to use the feminine energy of compassionate, feeling invitation or the more masculine energy of single-minded purpose and focus. In most life situations there will be a need to utilize both. In couples therapy I often highlight the opposite energies of mare and stallion and encourage partners to value them equally; achieving balance within the individual is equally important.

With Key Four the therapist helps the client explore issues of assertiveness and respectful persuasion; willingness to lead using clear and congruent communication; striking a balance of needs in mutually satisfying relationships; learning to turn toward the partner when miscommunication occurs, and to initiate repair attempts when misunderstanding damages the relationship. This is time to explore the "rock and roll" found within the activity of relationship, time to learn how to remain flexible and connected without sacrificing goals. This is active partnership with the horse.

For many clients assertiveness may have gone hand in hand with boundary infringement and a feeling of being used. For these clients therapy will go slower and it is imperative that facilitators have good intuition and discernment to maintain safety both physically and emotionally. At HEAL, relationship rituals are emphasized and clients learn to nurture attunement and limbic connection with the horse before trying to manipulate behavior.

Active work with the horse provides some of the most dynamic and structural aspects of the developing bond between client and horse, and the progression of therapy. By dynamic, I mean action-oriented, by structural I mean the human taking up the leadership position, with an agenda, in a persuasive way. As I facilitate these activities I depend on a brain circuit that all mammals enjoy, especially when they're young: PLAY.

Most of the research on this neural circuit refers to a specific kind of play, called rough-and-tumble play. An aspect of this neural circuit is that it can engage all of the other emotional circuits, in an atmosphere of safety and familiarity. The PLAY circuit has a special bio-evolutionary purpose for young mammals. It is through play that individual strengths and natural superiorities emerge, conferring a natural authority on those best equipped to serve as leaders. Humans and other mammals continue to play, and to refine social and family roles through play, throughout the lifespan.

Behavioral primes generated by the PLAY neural circuit include play signals and rituals, (which are to a large extent species-specific), rapid spurts of activity with animals taking turns, and spontaneous expressions of exuberance and engagement with the play partner. Dominant play partners will often modulate themselves in order to allow the weaker partner to win, hoping the partner will stay in the game.

Pain, excessive domination and fear end play.

Horses are playful, which we see all too rarely unless the horses are given some liberty and an enriched environment with opportunities for socialization, exploration and movement (Grandin, 2009; Jackson, 2010). A common all-purpose social game for horses is one that I call "Who Moves Whom?" This resembles a game of tag, often with a less dominant horse initiating through an act of sneaky disrespect to a friendly elder, who responds by "reprimanding." In geldings housed together, this often takes a modified form called "head sparring," which involves moving not the feet, but jousting with just the head and neck in order to avoid a threatened nip. In some herds, games develop such as mutual tugging on a stick. Another category of game involves the dynamic of harmonizing while excelling: racing, playing "scaredy-cat" together, or simply having a high headed trot down the runway on a cool day. *We as humans enter into these games and become part of the herd in every aspect of horsemanship.*

Key Four signals the beginning of action-oriented horse exercises in the development of EFPL, with a heightened potential for cathartic experience that creates a vividly experienced neural imprint. Key Four involves persuading the horse to engage in active play, or a training goal, initiating and making our requirements known through *clear and congruent communication*. In active work with horses, many layers of ambiguity in our body language and expressive demeanor are revealed. Clients learn skills for task negotiation and navigation of differences, with repair attempts when misunderstandings occur. The horse exercises in Key Four help the client feel safe in these relatively spontaneous experiences, which may not have been safe for them historically.

A fundamental skill for this Key is the client's ability to assume the Yang (or male) "driving" position. In classic equine family structure, this would be the herd stallion's position, his authority enforced by "the bite." An important role of the herd stallion is to scan outward for danger, and drive the herd to safety when predation threatens. This is in contrast to the charismatic position of the lead mare, who typically moves at the front of the herd. She must sense inward to the herd body, reading the needs of different horses who may be hungry, thirsty or needing a safe place to foal. Sensing this balance of needs, the lead mare strikes out with her experience and knowledge of their world. Trusting her experience and authority, the other horses follow. This requires finesse and it is called the drawing position. This is very limbic territory; the handler who can step into either (yang or yin) position will win the trust of the horse (and will also have a balanced psyche).

Encouraging the client to take the risks necessary for assertiveness without losing the sensitivity for their partner results in a profound sense of efficacy in relationship. Goals include clear and congruent communication, balance, mutual regulation and successful interdependency. The activities are exhilarating, and work well to integrate and balance the receptive and active, sensory and motor qualities, which might be called Yin and Yang.

Key Four allows clients to begin marrying the element necessary for goal achievement—focus—with a sensitive awareness necessary to protect connection. There will be friction at this point in therapy; what I call "the rub." As in any human relationship, resistance will show up when agenda becomes necessary. Incongruence in the human will result in the horse questioning determination and intent. If the person is too assertive, the horse will become shy. If the person is too kind, it may muddy the intent.

Prey animals never stray far from a sensing current and wide awareness. Human beings, like all predators, have the ability for intense concentration and selective focus. Dressage master Charles DeKunffy said, "The horse borrows the rider's focus, but to understand the horse the rider must expand his awareness. By joining their very different minds, both are improved." Both Yin and Yang are necessary for success in life and relationships.

TYPICAL EFPL ACTIVITIES FOR KEY FOUR

Successfully helping your clients navigate the activities of Key Four depends on a clear limbic connection, not just between client and horse, but also between therapist and client, and therapist (and/or horse specialist) and the horse. This allows for a richness of subtle communication between all parties, including the horse. Without such a connection, the horse tends to get confused as incongruities show up in the human participants, including the therapist at times.

It is not uncommon for the client to experience ambivalence and shame around issues of assertiveness or strength, a childhood wound that persists into adulthood. The client's ambivalence about being assertive may go underground as she attempts to follow the procedures for an active round pen session. The client will appear to be sending the horse all the right signals, yet the horse senses the inner doubt and becomes stuck, unresponsive to the client's signals. This should be regarded as communication to those who can understand—and the horse should trust the therapist to understand. If the therapist becomes too invested in agenda, the result may be escalating pressure on the horse to comply with the overt signals. This might exceed the boundaries of respectful negotiation. Resorting to force (i.e. causing fear or actual pain to the horse) is never helpful in a mental health therapy or education setting.

It's an important issue to explore, since activities that involve a strong yin-yang component are those that have a specific agenda or rules for play. Examples include advanced leading activities, longeing the horse on a line or at liberty, riding the horse, directing the horse through or over challenge obstacles. Key Four activities can include strategic, targeted training on certain horsemanship tasks (on ground or ridden).

It is critical to temper these activities with a bias toward relationship over outcome. Making the horse do what we want through force or intimidation does not equal the teaching of healthy relationship, nor does it model healthy relationship.

A picture is worth a thousand words. So I commonly introduce this active phase of the client's therapy work with a brief demonstration of the leadership dynamics that cause the horse's instinctive response to "join up." I describe the role of the lead mare, and demonstrate how she moves to the front, drawing the other horses with her by the power of attraction (the promise of need fulfillment). This is the Yin (female) position. The lead mare watches within the herd and anticipates the needs of herd members; she also has the experience and wisdom to know where these needs will be met. As I demonstrate I lay the rope over the horse's neck and continue in the leading position. Many horses will show a tendency to follow before peeling away. This is not join up.

I then explain that the stallion has a different role than the mare—generally speaking he watches outside of the herd for danger, and will drive the herd away from danger by herding them from behind. And he does this with the command that says, "If you don't move I'll bite your butt." This is the Yang (male) position. Seated in my personal power and confident in my horsemanship skills, I can demonstrate the light side of assertiveness, a strong yet friendly demeanor that is persuasive—commanding and encouraging at the same time. The right combination of clear and congruent driving (stallion energy), combined with a sensitive ability to see the horse's needs (lead mare energy), reliably causes the join up response within a short session even in horses that are not "trained" to do this. The "join up" response is an instinct of the horse's mammalian limbic brain. Join up represents the mechanics of herd structure.

Most clients I work with, youth to adult, learn to direct the horse in the round pen to work at different gaits (walk, trot, and canter), and change direction. The pace and energy can be modified to what the client is able to handle. When this can be managed by a client able to balance assertiveness and sensitivity, and sense their own body and the responses of the horse, the client and horse will achieve join up in most cases. Being able to take the "driving position" is an essential bit of limbic language; in order to drive the horse the client must master the cue that says, "I intend to bite your butt." At HEAL we employ principles that soften the join up process, making it more relational. For instance, we instruct clients to greet the horse in a friendly fashion before initiating play. And to always end the session in an honoring fashion, may the best teacher "win." May the relationship be strengthened by the activities.

With well socialized horses the essential rough and tumble game that horses play with each other called "who moves whom?" can also be called "who leads?" It is quite clear at times that the horse knows these games much better than the people know them. Herd structure and relational dynamics shine through every action in these games that are played on the ground, often with the horse at liberty (or on a lead or lunge line).

Many challenge exercises with horses can involve leadership, and so the dynamics of Yin and Yang can be explored by meeting other challenges, such as sending the horse through a challenging obstacle (over a tarp, or a jump, or up a bank and back down). As the relationship with the horse develops, there will be innumerable opportunities to increase the horse's trust in the human handler through meeting challenges together and by balancing Yin and Yang. An increasing sense of harmony will be evident as the client finds greater ease in balancing assertiveness with sensitivity to their partner. It is especially in meeting shared challenges that mutual regulation between horse and human as a team becomes critical.

For clients that ride there will be natural challenges that represent personal efficacy for different stages of therapy. For some clients this may be cantering on the horse, for a number it might be taking a trail ride, or riding bareback. Most activities undertaken with a horse require a balance of persuasive driving and sensitive leading. The confident horseperson allows the horse to lead at moments as well, in a back and forth dance.

◈ EFPL HORSE ACTIVITY ◈
Join Up First Liberty Active Exercise

In the horse herd, the natural spatial language of "who moves whom?" and "who is drawn together with whom?" are the clearest expressions of the "limbic language" within the herd, defining the internal herd structure. Understanding the mechanics and the limbic dynamics of "join up" is, I believe, essential to EFPL. As an EFPL facilitator, we encourage you to invest in your own learning and skill improvement to become competent in this fundamental language of the equine limbic system. This is especially true if the facilitator is going to work with unfamiliar horses. Do not attempt this activity with clients until you can reliably create the join up response with lightness and accuracy. It should not be necessary to force the horse; forcing the horse to join up has no place in mental health therapy or the teaching of social-emotional skills for humans.

Procedures for join up session:

1. Stand outside the round pen with the target horse and *establish your own baseline* and arousal number, noting specific sensations or affects. (Perhaps, do this facing away from the horse and then toward the horse.)

2. Notice the details of the environment from the perspective of the horse. Take a moment to send your energy out toward the horse; this is your 'meet the herd' moment.

3. Go into the round pen with the target horse. Keep your mind balanced and your focus on the horse (even if he seems to be focused toward something else), without losing your awareness of your own sensations and details of the environment. Keep your eyes and mind (both limbic and neo-cortex) focused on the horse. Notice your breathing. If your arousal level is at an eight or above then self-regulate to something less than eight. (Doesn't matter if the arousal is plus or minus, get into and stay within the window of tolerance.)

The remainder of these steps depends on what the horse does. What he does is a function of who he is, his history and his primary interest at the time in the present environment.

4. A well-gentled horse, by this time, may come toward you with limbic curiosity. When he does, don't move toward him, but do move SLOWLY (horse time) away. Back away and *draw the horse* toward you. Allow the horse to catch you, touching or nearly touching you, smelling instead of touching. JOIN UP.

But what if the horse has never been caught? Then walk toward him with your arousal in the window of tolerance and *drive him* if he isn't already trying to avoid you. Then proceed with the following steps:

5. When the horse tries to run around the perimeter of the round pen to escape you, then block his path with the least energy you need to contain the horse, and the least change of your own position necessary to contain the horse.

6. When he stops and looks at you STOP; drop your energy and arousal level and maybe even turn away—that STOP is his reinforcement cue telling the horse that this connection may be OK after all.

7. Once he has connected with you, you can draw him for Join Up or you can get closer by every cycle of approach and retreat when he points his head at you. Then you can halter him.

Join up is a limbic, three fold connection: resonance, regulation, and finally revision.

⁀ EFPL HORSE ACTIVITY ⁀
Horsemanship Exercises in Energy and Intention

Natural horsemanship is the philosophy of working with horses by appealing to their instincts (brainstem) and herd-social instincts (limbic system). It involves techniques built on the natural communication in the herd in order to build a partnership that closely resembles the relationships that exist between horses. For thousands of years these elements of energetic flexibility and control have been utilized by the most highly skilled trainers. The horse may at first be confused or distressed by seemingly mixed signals, but by the finish of the exercise the horse will be calm, feel safe and exhibit greater courage and understanding.

1. *Raising energy combined with intention for the horse to stay still.* The objective is for the horse to become attuned to the handler's intention (for the horse to stand still) while the handler strikes the ground with a great deal of force using the stick and string. The horse should be trained for this activity and the facilitator must be able to demonstrate (for the client or the horse's sake). If the client cannot manage their arousal, few horses will stand still. At least, that is the case with our horses at HEAL! This works best on a lead line, starting with low-intensity rhythmic pressure. Build intensity gradually.

2. *Energetic departure from the lightest signal.* This is like a sister exercise to the one above (horse to remain standing still in presence of strong, activating stimuli). In this exercise, the intention and energy of the handler are high, the energy expenditure is low. The horse is given the expectation of standing ready, and moving off promptly with energy that is high and calm. The perfect, prompt departure from a standstill shows both respect and trust; and it comes from practice and more practice—some of it awkward and vulnerable. This exercise can be on lead line or at liberty in the round pen.

3. *Desensitizing.* Horses are creatures of caution and flight—this is their survival strategy. Working on the lead line, it can be very rich for the client to work through the horse's innate and instinctive caution about certain stimuli: flags, tarps, crossing through a curtain of plastic strips, or crossing challenging obstacles (tarp or small jump).

Working through these challenges is rich in relational currency (trust, respect, and willingness) and metaphorical value. The Key Four active exercises are extremely multi-dimensional and build integration of bottom up and top down processing.

ꕥ EFPL PRACTICE TIP ꕤ
How to Play With, Instead of Working a Horse

- The most studied play circuit is for "rough and tumble" play. While many mammals roll and pin each other, horses commonly play "who moves whom."

- Play involves imagination and cognition as well as emotion, even for horses.

- No PAIN!! (At least not intentional.) And NOT truly scary. Fear poisons play.

- Pushing the horse to the point of sweaty fatigue is not play.

- Youthfulness and vigor influence the length of play cycles. In general, horses will play hard for 20-30 minutes maximum, usually much shorter than that.

- It must be mutual: win-win. A research-supported ratio: less than 30% wins = no fun.

- In play, we exercise all of our emotional circuitry (all other flavors of emotion) in a container of safety and goodwill.

- Responsiveness to others' signals, conscious and unconscious.

- Voluntary restraint of the strongest partner to insure participation of weaker playmate.

- Pleasurable and uninhibited; characterized by joyful expressions and exchanges. Even rats laugh! www.youtube.com/watch?v=j-admRGFVNM

"Humans are the only species that can turn their play into work!" Leigh Shambo

Every species has their own play signals that are used to initiate a game. Horses often attempt to initiate play through harmless but noticeable acts of disrespect, for instance a nudge. Horses buck out of playfulness and often rear up when they are playing. It is wonderful to see horses play in this way while being careful of a person's physical space.

Our Arabian mare Dixsi was therapy horse for "Sue" during sessions at HEAL. Rediscovering play had been an important goal of therapy for this young woman whose childhood was shaped by loss of her mother, care of siblings, and functioning as a little adult from a young age. Through their work together, Sue developed an especially loving and exuberant relationship with our therapy horse Dixsi. During one session of ground play in the round pen, Dixsi reared high, keeping a respectful distance and manner, three times in a row! Then with perfect gentleness stepped up to nuzzle Sue, who got the message: "Get on with it!" Dixsi was completely obedient and tuned in; Sue was flushed and radiant with positive arousal, while still tuned in to Dixsi.

~ KEY FOUR Vignette ~
Tina in PTSD group session four

During group session four (of seven), the girls handled their horses on lead lines out in a field, each girl challenged to hold her horse's attention on the lush, tempting grass. Tina was struggling that day, but not with Beau. She was mad at everyone wearing a human costume, meanwhile ignoring Beau who waited beside her. He, unlike the other horses, was not tempted to graze. He looked worried—was he able to sense Tina's foul mood?

We were exploring assertiveness with Key Four, Yin and Yang—and the work on "Not Grazing" is prelude to an exercise called "Knocking on the Door." To "Knock on the Door" each girl, individually, releases her horse into the large outdoor round pen, first allowing it to graze at liberty, then approaching the horse to request its full attention, without touching. On this day, the first four girls were successful in commanding (not forcing) their horse to return to them.

Then it was Tina's turn. Several times, Tina "knocked" and Beau "answered," but each time just as he turned toward Tina, she was already looking away with a shrug. Beau became confused, then less responsive. Time started to drag. The agency van arrived and was waiting to take the girls back to the mental health center. I felt myself pushing, unwilling to let her "fail"—so I backed off, leaving it up to her, and Beau. I could let them be accountable to each other.

Suddenly I felt Tina get mad (in my gut I felt it!), then she shot me a look that could kill. She marched toward Beau. His head snapped up. And this time, Tina responded to him by softening her energy, letting her breath out, and stepping backward (the energetic "draw" that invites the horse). Beau came toward her, quietly and carefully.

Tina did not speak to me as the girls boarded the van back to the agency. Later, in conference with her agency therapist, I learned that Tina had reasons for being mad at the world: another contact with her abuser, a family member. I also learned that Tina was angry with me for "not letting her off the hook." The group session had been difficult—for all of us including Beau—but this session marked a turning point for Tina.

In the remaining group sessions, Tina revealed herself as an active partner with Beau and also more willing to interact with peers in the group. Things didn't always go smoothly, but we muddled and felt our way. In the process, relationships were strengthened.

Tina was finally with us.

More about Tina in Chapter 7 …

MORE ABOUT KEY FOUR: THE PLAY OF YIN AND YANG

All predators have a strong desire to achieve goals. A common house cat is a mammal that demonstrates the predator's drive to hunt. This has shaped the nervous system for the focused determination needed—imagine a cat waiting for hours outside the mouse hole.

A rabbit does not get pleasure from the seeking hunt but in finding safety. The rabbit's nervous system—similar to the much larger horse—is consumed by self-protection. Prey animals let the environment influence behavior. The prey animal is a constant sensor, inhibited and reluctant to take risks.

Human beings are sometimes considered the ultimate predator residing at the top of the food chain. But are we really? Though human beings as a species are predators, we have diverse life experiences that condition us to focus on seeking or sensing. It can be hard to find and nurture balance. Both Yang and Yin are necessary for success in life and relationships.

Working with horses, however, allows us to cultivate better balance. As we discover the best ways to influence and connect with a high sensing prey animal, our ability to be sensitive to the needs of others will also grow.

Prey animals never stray far from a sensing current and wide awareness. Human beings, as a species, can be thought of as "super predators" with the ability for intense concentration and powerful selective focus; though we should not forget that even humans may all too easily become prey. Many trauma survivors struggle with the smooth integration of sensing and acting capacities. The active work with horses allows the EFPL client to safely practice highly integrating activities with a naturally connective partner who wants them to succeed.

Of course, the practice does not always go smoothly. We encourage clients to muddle their way though awkward moments, trusting in mammal-to-mammal communication. The horse is always trying to find the client's true intent. Through these moments, the client should feel safe at all times and empowered by what they have learned from the previous keys. The client can experience freedom from impulsive reacting, shed old patterns, and embrace the right to choose how to act and what to believe about a situation even in action moments.

Figure 6. Schematic illustration of bottom-up (yin) and top-down (yang) processes.

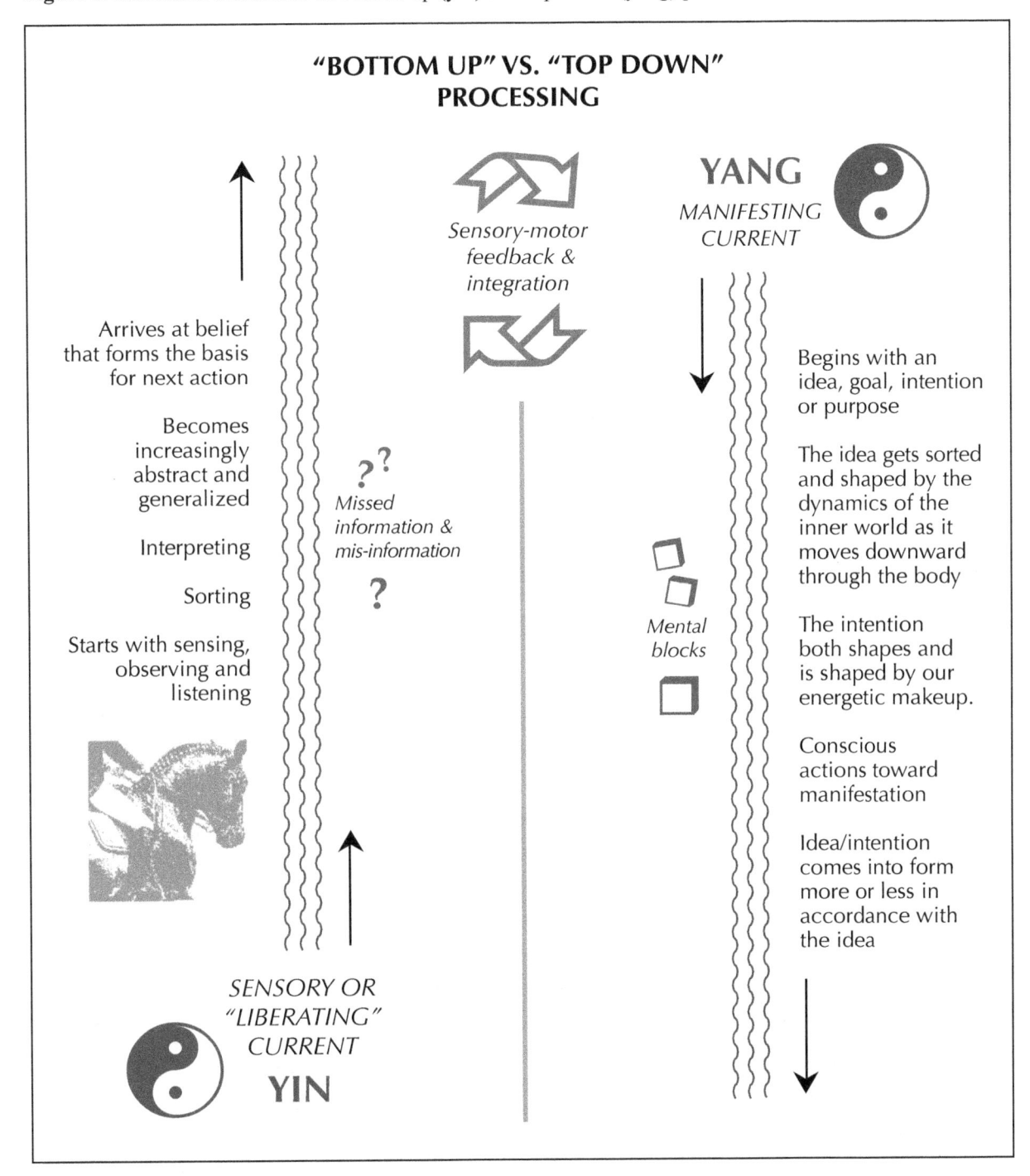

"BOTTOM UP" VS. "TOP DOWN" PROCESSING

Sensory-motor feedback & integration

YANG
MANIFESTING CURRENT

Arrives at belief that forms the basis for next action

Becomes increasingly abstract and generalized

Interpreting

Sorting

Starts with sensing, observing and listening

Missed information & mis-information

Mental blocks

Begins with an idea, goal, intention or purpose

The idea gets sorted and shaped by the dynamics of the inner world as it moves downward through the body

The intention both shapes and is shaped by our energetic makeup.

Conscious actions toward manifestation

Idea/intention comes into form more or less in accordance with the idea

SENSORY OR "LIBERATING" CURRENT
YIN

76 THE LISTENING HEART

HEAL workshop students using a modified join up activity to encourage limbic joining with the horse.

This student has lots of horse experience and was able to become more experimental, playful and full of feeling with the horse.

Photo 4. *Driving position.*

Photo 5. *The moment of drawing.*

Photo 6. *Joining and mirroring.*

This student possesses little horse experience, but the horsemanship is simple when the person is clear and congruent. When the horse joins him he becomes absorbed in studying her.

Photo 7. *Driving.*

Photo 8. *Inviting join up. Drawing.*

Photo 9. *What now? Mirroring.*

Photos used with permission.

Chapter Seven

The Fifth Key: New Pathways (in the Brain!)

"Neural plasticity has the power to produce more flexible but also more rigid behaviors ... Some of our most stubborn habits and disorders are products of our plasticity ... It is by understanding both the positive and negative effects of plasticity that we can truly understand the extent of human possibilities."

Norman Doidge
The Brain That Changes Itself:
Stories of Personal Triumph from the Frontiers of Brain Science

THERAPEUTIC STRATEGY IN KEY FIVE: ASK, SEEK AND KNOCK IN PRACTICE

The mind has something in common with a parachute: both work best when open. It takes honesty to know oneself, and effort to put that knowing to use in life. Change may be even more challenging for many of our clients whose biology, beliefs and behaviors have been shaped by tragic experience. It is now evident that brains change throughout life, and positive change can occur as the result of focused activities and thought. Scientists no longer explain the brain in mechanical terms such as "hard wired" but with the newer reality of *neuroplasticity*.

Neuroscientist Norman Doidge tells us, "… that the damaged brain can often reorganize itself so that when one part fails, another can often substitute; that if brain cells die, they can at times be replaced; that many "circuits" and even basic reflexes that we think are 'hardwired' are not." (Doidge, 2007, p. xix) Neuroplasticity is at work in the brain when one learns a new skill, such as playing the piano. To take it one step further, current science shows that "… Imagination is not irrelevant; when sufficiently focused, it engages the same sensory and motor functions as physical activity (Doidge, 2007, Ch. 8).

Using Key Five, the therapist and client explore the affective domain of imagination, seeking and searching. Some clients will feel terrified as they practice new behaviors; others may find it exciting. Some clients may have been impulsive to begin with and are learning to look before they leap. Younger clients may have little self-awareness of their change process. Yet all of them are building fragile new pathways in their brains. New pathways need repetition, practice, and most of all, change needs to be motivated and rewarded!

With Key Five we direct attention to the brain's all-purpose motivation system. Panksepp calls this brain affective system SEEKING, and it is employed in searching for rewards of all kinds. All mammals have this innate circuitry, which is not about the rewards, but the excitement of searching them out. Animals prefer to work or search for food rather than have it simply given (Grandin, 2009, 275-76). The behavioral primes embedded in the SEEKING neural circuit include sniffing, investigating, and all manner of species-specific utilitarian behaviors designed to achieve desires. The SEEKING system primes an organism to make causal associations and seek meaning (especially in humans). If it is not tempered by commitment to the evidence, thinking influenced by SEEKING can become unrealistic, or even delusional.

What does SEEKING look like in the horse? In the wild, horses must SEEK for their daily needs, covering many miles to find new grazing and visit waterholes or foaling grounds. Wild or domestic, horses need to move a lot (Jackson, 2010) and like to investigate their surroundings. Safety is always paramount to horses, which illustrates a prioritization of brain circuits favoring survival over rewards. When horses feel safe, it is easy to amplify their natural curiosity and inspire SEEKING. Careful, positive shaping enables reasoned choice for horses and people (Grandin, 2009, p. 129).

SEEKING has been called "a kind of master emotion" (Grandin, 2009, p.7). It has also been theorized by many that the SEEKING brain circuits contain the spiritual impulse, as well as sexual impulse, and impulses for other important life fulfillment activities as well. When two beings are related by a SEEKING impulse, they are in mutual aid to each other. Dominance is not so important if each is making a contribution that the other values. This helps us understand the notion of an accepted leader versus dominant leader (Rashid, 2000, p. 37).

Key Five activities highlight the power of the successful bond between two mammals. Activities such as running with the horse, dancing with the horse, facing obstacles together and succeeding create vivid, memorable and unique neural imprints. These combine high positive arousal, with the reassurance of a regulating partner, performing feats together with flexible and realistic expectations of each other. Experience with the previous Keys (One through Four) help create the trust and flexibility *to turn toward each other when things go slightly off course*. It is up to the clinician to create bridges that enable the client to translate new, adaptive behaviors to their human environments to create "a home run!"

Humans can run into a variety of problems with the modulation of this SEEKING circuit. The work of Panksepp and others shows SEEKING to be appetitive rather than consummatory in nature—meaning that consumption (or goal attainment) turns the SEEKING off, at least temporarily. The energized anticipatory excitement induced by this circuit can become addictive and it is a player in the development of substance and behavioral addictions. The goal-focused narrowing of cortical capacities can cause the seeking to become a predominant concern, crowding out other rewards. This was described by one student as "PANIC SEEKING." She learned to sense when her relentless SEEKING was driven by thwarted attachment needs. The dilemma, stemming from unresolved history: complete merging versus abandonment and unmet need. In this case SEEKING becomes a tortuous yearning that can't fulfill its promise, consuming but never filling up.

It is important to remember that frustration of the SEEKING behaviors can lead to aggression. This is true across the seeking spectrum, from seekers of religious truth to type A personalities to the emotionally immature person who craves a fantasy instead of a real person. This can be another topic of valuable clinical work within this affective domain, especially for clients with low frustration tolerance and attention deficits. Horses will reliably reward people who are consistent in relationship—those who can soothe themselves and be responsible for their own emotions.

The power of this SEEKING circuit has fueled the vast human appetite for discovery and invention. Seeking is related to hope and to interest in life and sense of purpose. Engagement of the seeking circuit gives powerful support to therapy. Seeking can be fun. Seeking keeps the imagination alive. Seeking may even have its own force or energy of attraction. Seeking can also be fragile, vulnerable to disruption, ambivalence and extinction.

Most of us are SEEKING much of the time. Panksepp describes a SEEKING neural circuit that maintains engagement, in order to opportunistically capitalize on fortuitous events and follow promising threads. True seeking usually entails vulnerability and risk. Many clients habitually underestimate themselves, avoid risk and seek safety more than gain. Other clients are impulsive seekers, so focused on possible outcomes that they ignore red flags.

Balance in the SEEKING circuit helps the client recognize the difference between fear and vulnerability. Vulnerability, they are learning, is an ally, and calculated risk is a necessity to growth. The client begins to trust their own resilience. The capacity to trust others and seek limbic connection increases. More positive emotional circuits such as PLAY and SEEKING have a magnetic effect in the client's life by attracting serendipities, coincidences and synchronicity. In truth, these emotions attract other people and make it easy for them to be supportive. These attributes are the norm in a life characterized by expectant seeking, faith, and intentional vulnerability. With Key Five, New Pathways, the client has a new opportunity for experiencing the magnetic power of a balanced SEEKING circuit.

TYPICAL EFPL ACTIVITIES FOR KEY FIVE: ASK, SEEK AND KNOCK IN PRACTICE

A wide array of EFPL activities can focus on imagination and help the client explore the SEEKING circuit in themselves and their equine partner. What is chosen depends on client characteristics, treatment goals and the stage of therapy. If an EFPL practitioner has been exploring the Keys sequentially (such as in group treatment), the client may be entering the culmination stage of therapy. Exercising the imagination within the context of an already developed relationship between human and horses makes the Key Five EFPL exercises especially powerful.

Temple Grandin explored the shared characteristics of autistic people and animals in her fascinating best seller, *Thinking in Pictures*. The book explores what Grandin discovered as an animal scientist and a person with autism: animals think in pictures. Horses have a strong tendency to "pick up" and "follow" a picture. This is especially true when the shared limbic connection is one of safety, expected success, and anticipation of shared pleasure, such as the human and the horse have experienced in mutual engagement of PLAY neural circuitry.

Visualization improves all partnership activities between horse and person. A simple join-up exercise in the round pen can be expanded by encouraging the client to hold (focus on) an imagined image. Standing beside the horse, the client tunes into the breathing and attentional dynamics, making limbic connection with the horse. Then, the client imagines walking with the horse (or other maneuver), not as a verbal construct or command, but as palpable body image, or a sensual picture. By remaining receptive to the horse's signals the most common outcome is that within minutes client and horse suddenly begin walking together! It should not be surprising, because this is the way that it happens horse to horse and humans, after all, are mammals too.

Horses have a way of grounding us when our imagination becomes too grandiose. Common sense and realistic assessment is as important as unfettered imagination. A wave of escalating positive emotion may become a case of Rose Colored Glasses, and disconnection within relationship is the result. A client can be so focused on their own imaginative experience that they miss signals from the horse that communicate confusion, indifference, or frustration. Remaining connected to our partner is critical, whether horse or human. It is important that clients learn to "reality test" and to examine values and goals in light of everyday actions. Do they match?

Testing the durability of the bond with the horse—stretching it!—is central to this stage of therapy and makes the bond even stronger. So if the horse will follow you around a small pen, will he continue to follow in the larger arena? In the presence of food, or other horses? Can you keep him following outside of the arena, with the opportunity for complete liberty and the temptation of green grass and endless exploration? Can you imagine keeping the bond of security and trust intact while you both get your needs met? *This* is deep limbic work!

Liberty and lightness—the fruits of partnership—characterize a stage of therapy where the client has put some work into building a relationship with the horse. Grooming the horse at liberty, navigating an obstacle course with the horse at liberty, dancing with the horse to music, or running and playing with the horse free in arena or pasture. Horse dancing is an imaginative activity in which the client and horse engage in free play in the arena or round pen to music that can be impromptu, or in some cases selected or created by the client.

❧ EFPL HORSE ACTIVITY ❧
Contemplative Time Spent with the Horses

For clients who need help listening to their inner voice: A fairly easy technique for rediscovering intuition is to practice mindful breathing and self awareness while sitting quietly in the presence of one or more horses. When practical, this is often a good way to open or close a session of office psychotherapy. Intuition is a quiet voice, often overpowered by more "rational" or so-called "false self" voices—the inner critic. Some clients take a journal with them. The therapist should sit quietly nearby, patiently engaged in noticing the client's non-verbal signs and any responses from the horse, and to help the client mark time and close the session with time to debrief the experience and explore the client's perceptions. At HEAL, there are times when clients are allowed to spend time on their own with horses before or after a session.

During contemplative time, the horses may be drawn into proximity with the client or not. Sometimes they do notable things, such as nuzzling a client's notebook or standing over them protectively. Other times they may explore on their own or nap nearby. Either way, the client has an opportunity to notice internal questions and judgments in the moment, while staying tuned in to their own sensing device, the body.

❧ EFPL HORSE ACTIVITY ❧
Horse Decoration & Commemoration

Creative arts may be used throughout therapy with many clients, and these have a special place as client and therapist explore Key Five and move into the culmination state of therapy. Interactive activities are imaginative, creative and honoring—such as painting on the horse and weaving beads, feathers and ribbons into the mane and tail. Water-based, non-toxic paints that wash off easily (such as those used in face and body painting) work best.

Clients have written poetry and letters to the horses, created paintings and shields to help them reinforce, represent and bridge the learning from EFPL sessions. These activities provide important reinforcement for the new neural pathways. Decorating and honoring the horse or horses worked with during therapy can combine well with spontaneously created rituals such as a self-designed parade with a grand entry, the human carrying a flag while mounted or leading the horse.

❧ EFPL HORSE ACTIVITY ☙
Horse Dancing

Horse dancing makes a lovely culmination activity, which, for safety and effectiveness, *depends on the learning in the previous Keys*. It opens up freely moving energy and helps clients connect with their bodies in pleasurable and functional ways. However, its great strengths are also its risks. The EFPL clinician should feel sure of the following things: that the client feels confident moving the horse in the round pen; that the client has skills in self-regulation and the ability to stay grounded if the horse becomes very active or playful. Some clients will need more structure than others in the form of instruction or, in rare cases, the presence of a more skilled horse handler beside them. The use of music and drumming is a powerful influence on the brainstem, an important consideration with some types of clients. Many clients at HEAL benefit from light, harmonic music, who might not benefit from heavier or more intense selections.

Movement is both revealing and helpful, and while some clients need to free up their movement many of our serious clinical cases need more organization and structure to their bodies and their movement. For this I have found that it's best to have the horse and handler joined by a lead line, giving them an extra structure by which the horse can help organize the person. Music can be played with good effect in the background of almost any horse activity, and the horses often seem to enjoy it as well!

❧ EFPL HORSE ACTIVITY ☙
Journey and Archetype Activities

No adventure is without its risks, or without the potential rewards we earn only by risking, by becoming vulnerable. When we invent games and challenges for the client (which can be done on horseback, or as ground activities with the client and horse as partners) we awaken the archetypal by creating a theatre of the imagination. The horse will join in. For example, when you ask a client to imagine how the queen (or the herd leader) would walk (posture, breathing, stature, and attitude), you will almost always see the horse mirror these changes and accord the person more respect. Other games include finding toy animals to be collected in a centrally placed "stable" (bucket), retrieving a hat or a cape, crossing obstacles, or imagining a journey.

Horses not only respond to our inner pictures and archetypes, they actually stimulate them. On horseback, we share in the majesty of the horse's natural bearing and experience a fantasy-like transformation. We are stronger and more capable with a horse, able to gallop off into a better reality. We are more than "just" a man or woman in the company of a horse.

Journey activities can be invented in many different scenarios and are helpful for working with the client's self-narratives; they integrate the sense of meaning and self-in-relationship. One such activity invites the client to identify significant points on their life journey, turning points, important relationships marking periods of personal history. Then, the client chooses specific points in and around the horse arena, to correspond to specific times of difficulty, change, hopefulness. These places can be marked as "stations" using the ground poles commonly found in horse arenas.

Each station should be constructed to include the horse partner who will be along for the journey. The stations can be elaborated on to more vividly represent the memories. A confusing time might be represented by a maze or labyrinth of poles that the client and horse will navigate together. A time of relative peace can be represented by putting a chair inside the poles marking the station, where the client may rest awhile with the horse. Stations that require effort, such as trot-over poles or even a jump, a reward stop with actual horse treats, or having to confront a scary object such as crossing a tarp with the horse—all of these will provide rich opportunities to enter into the client's world as the journey is put in place.

The client selects a horse companion for the journey. The selection is made on the basis of resonance or "rightness" based on body scanning. At this point the facilitator becomes a witness from a relative distance, allowing client and horse to journey together through the stations. As this activity often occurs somewhat later in therapy, the client may have deepened into relationship with one horse, or worked with several. Sometimes horse and client give us a surprise – a new thread created by spontaneous resonance.

The horse's response to stepping inside each station will reflect their feel for the client's affective state. Their response may also be based on the actual challenges or conditions within a station. Because each station also represents a remembered point in time, the client may be able to access new skills and understandings that he or she holds at this point in time, but did not have then. All of these are rich therapeutic topics that will help to illuminate a client's self-narrative, giving opportunities for revision, for feeling supported in the present, for recognizing some of the gifts of the past as well as an opportunity to let go of the pain.

In therapy I help clients to identify archetypes they have been unconsciously assuming —the Martyr or Victim, for example. By Key Five, clients have a greater capacity for objectivity and honesty and it is a good time to identify possible archetypes and the light and shadow inherent in each one. When one can become conscious of archetype they can begin examining motive, intention and boundaries in a new way. Even a positive model such as The Hero has a shadow side. For example, one can be overly invested in a relationship to "save" someone (who may not want to be saved). Archetypes are birthed from our family of origin, unique personal make-up, and experience. They can be a source of important insight.

Children naturally understand and move within the realm of archetype and it is a commonly used story pattern in youth literature. A common theme is the hero going on a journey, encountering difficulty, and learning something important along the way. Life is an adventure for the young. Over time, personality matures and becomes set. The mid-life crisis is often a spirited attempt to shed the rigid self, and find meaning in the contributions of an authentic self. When this does not occur, depression and withdrawal are common symptoms.

EFPL HORSE ACTIVITY
Clicker Training

At HEAL, in addition to a foundation of natural training and round pen methods, we like to train our horses using a clicker for certain reward-based specific tasks. Tasks can include touching a particular object, retrieving a small cone, or discriminating colors. The "click" (we use a unique, dedicated verbal sound rather than the handheld clicker) is a sound that signals, "Hey! You just earned a reward!" This gives clients a chance to see the horses operating out of their cortical centers, as the emotional circuit SEEKING prompts problem solving and creativity.

The equine specialist can develop basic clicker skills in the herd, by "charging the clicker" and teaching some simple tricks. Clients and visitors to HEAL are often surprised to watch the horses retrieve items, follow a target, or quickly learn something new when they are positively motivated. It is wonderful experiential practice for exploring what motivates behavior and how to effectively reward.

Rewards are an important topic for family dynamics in parent-child or couples therapy. In both situations perfectly rational adults fail to adequately reward the behavior they wanted and have been asking for. Moods tend to get stuck in negative and our mind gets made up because of our mood. For example (said sarcastically): "I see you finally took the garbage out—it's about time." Such a remark is meant to continue punishing the partner rather than accomplish what one really wants!

Training with the clicker relies on operant conditioning and positive reinforcement. What's important to understand about the conditioning process is how it "teaches" all parts of the brain, awakening the basic SEEKING impulse in the brainstem; strengthening the limbic connection between human and horse; and activating the cortex as the horse builds cognitive pathways for learning. This is very different from conditioning using negative reinforcement, because it activates the SEEKING brain circuit. It is important to understand that the "pressure" applied in a natural horsemanship approach can be very subtle indeed, so let me be clear that I am not saying one is better. By understanding both negative and positive reinforcement we are better able to understand where each fits, for training the horse or for EFPL. The "click" is a bridging cue that makes reward-based training much more precise, helping all animals learn faster and with more confidence.

The horse must be prepared in advance using a foundation of classical conditioning to "charge the clicker," which readily translates to simple operant tasks, such as lowering the head. Trick training, or handling the horse as he performs tasks he is trained to do requires feel, timing, and understanding. The horse may become demanding, necessitating boundary setting. There are decisions about how high to hold the standards. A high level of observation skills and empathy is engaged in order to respond in a helpful way when the horse is becoming discouraged (extinction). Many clients seem willing to 'give away the store,' not asking much in return for the horse's attention. It is liberating and empowering to learn that the horse respects and is actively attracted to congruence and high standards.

Photos 10-11. *David is coaching Eva Balzer, a HEAL Facilitator Training graduate, in clicker training. Dixsi will fetch the plastic cone and return it to the handler. Photos used with permission.*

Like natural horsemanship and liberty training, clicker training requires an investment to learn and practice with the horses in the therapy herd. It must be thoughtfully incorporated into selected activities in which students are training specific tasks. We do not advocate rewarding the horses for standard respectful behavior, or using rewards to gain the horse's attention or join up. When such issues come up and clients want to over-rely on food rewards, EFPL provides a relationship laboratory from which rich learning and new choices can result.

✎ KEY FIVE Vignette ✎
Linda—Culmination stage of individual EFPL

Linda attended therapy at HEAL for more than a year with me and the horses. During that time her self-hatred, anger, and defensiveness—held physically as well as emotionally in her body—relaxed. Both anxiety and depression dropped considerably when Linda became better able to work with her own emotions, by using the Six Keys. But change was not always easy. One area of significant challenge involved her relationship with her mother, who had long been a domineering and trivializing presence in Linda's life. After learning to navigate respectful boundaries with a thousand-pound horse, Linda observed that every interaction with her mom left her drained and defensive. So she limited her time with Mom.

In addition to ending patterns that no longer served her, Linda was learning to step into the vulnerability of new relationships. With the horses, she was able to practice the fine art of positive imagination, balanced with realistic expectations. Linda still enjoyed working a lot with Cloud, who she experienced as very strong and very gentle and safe. Linda had to match Cloud's strength without becoming domineering and dismissive of his feelings. One day, Linda and Cloud walked all over the HEAL Ranch with just a neck rope, a single line draped loosely around his neck with no pressure. Linda's confidence in Cloud was spontaneous, flexible and effective. This was the kind of connection she longed for but had never experienced.

More about Linda in Chapter 8 …

Tina in PTSD group session 6

Tina was truly with us after her difficult fourth session. In the sixth session, the adolescent group took a hike with the horses 'in hand' (on lead lines). The excitement was contagious. The horses were on high alert, with "their girls" out in the wide world. Key Five, New Pathways, feels quite literal in this activity! Tina did not remain unmoved by the sunny day; her shoulders opened and her legs worked in the long grass. A watchful yet obedient Beau marched in tandem with her. In the line of walking horses, the hoofbeats felt like a drum. Exhilaration was high; it was balanced by the grounded calmness of good horsemanship.

At the apex of our circuit around the barn two deer burst from the bushes and ran right through the line of horses, toward the neighboring woods! The horses STARTLED but stood fast by their girls, including Beau with Tina. I watched as Beau checked in with Tina just after this occurrence—a concerned nod toward Tina, a sniff. Tina carefully laid her cheek on Beau's back. It was the first time I saw her express tenderness toward Beau, who had been tender with Tina all along.

More about Tina in Chapter 8 …

MORE ABOUT KEY FIVE: NEW PATHWAYS

For clients who have never imagined something outside their current situation, it can be life changing to experience a partner responding to a focused picture in one's imagination. The power we hold in our connections to others is the ability to change ourselves; no one can force change on another individual. But by focusing on what we want, on positive pictures, a miracle is free to happen. The future of a relationship can be changed with the power of imagination.

SEEKING has been called the master emotion for its vast motivational powers.

Clicker training strengthens the limbic bond in many ways. I'm surprised at the amount of prejudice that comes up about clicker training. In fact, I used to have some unfounded fears myself—such as that the horse will only want to work for food, etc. The clicker can give the horse confidence that he is doing the right thing when he faces his fears. Once the clicker is charged, i.e., the click sound is conditioned, it becomes a positive trigger encoded in the amygdale. While negative triggers, such as trauma cues, cause the nervous system to immediately revert to fight-or-flight, the clicker signals the impending reward of successful seeking—an immensely rewarding affective state.

Most of our horses are trained in simple tricks, such as touching a cone or a ball on the end of the stick that we can move about. A few of our horses are trained to pick things up, find hidden objects or discriminate one object from another. These activities allow the client to watch their partner (the horse) think at his own speed while motivated. Sometimes this is surprisingly fast (the horse might anticipate or be offering behaviors even before asked); other times it is slow, especially if a safety concern interferes (an unidentified noise outside the arena). Mostly, horse time is measured, and it never loses sight of the wide awareness that is essential to safety.

Archetypes: Frieda "the Queen"

At HEAL the Queen of the horse herd is my long-time friend and teacher, Frieda. Most clients readily intuit Frieda's queenly signals and many find her intimidating. Invariably, Frieda will avoid or snub the client who holds false self beliefs related to ability and/or self-worth. After all, she does not consort with commoners. However, when the client dares to approach Frieda with confidence—as a fellow Queen or King—it is interesting to note her response. She willingly engages with those who will claim their own worth. Though now well into her twenties, Frieda remains a strong archetype that has helped many clients step into a royal destiny. In truth, she is the strong lead mare of our small herd.

Archetypes: Gem "the Mother"

On the other hand, our small sturdy mare Gem, now around 40 years old, is our most gentle and generous horse, a highly maternal archetype although she has never had a foal. Gem often chooses, or is chosen by, the youngest, most fearful clients, or those torn by loss and grief. Gem frequently nickers to humans (the gentle voice used by horses for affectionate greeting). Gem is the first to investigate youngsters, be it a human client or a new puppy. When human children work with or ride Gem, her face shows tenderness, and her careful feet show the responsibility that she feels. Watching Gem over the years, I've noticed that she also knows how to take care of herself. People assume that she is "easy" and will do "anything for anybody." Not necessarily true! Gem is spirited and sensitive, and she knows how to hang out the 'not open for therapy' sign on certain days.

Renowned horse trainer Klaus Ferdinand Hempfling (2004, pp. 72-127) discusses equine character archetypes in his book, *What Horses Reveal*. The archetypes he describes are complex, "... a never ending story: nature and manner, likes and dislikes, and mental, physical and spiritual characteristics." (p. 72). Far beyond a personality sketch that predicts how trainable the horse is, these character descriptions are full of light and shadow: "That which appears to be stubbornness is in truth the expression of independent existence ... "

What kind of character are you?

As human clients come to understand horses as the complex characters that they are, it becomes possible for them to explore these complexities within themselves. It takes imagination and interest to move beyond value judgments of right and wrong, good or bad. Human or horse, each of us is a unique combination of innate temperament, our experiences and formative bonds within family and society, and our determination about what it means. The level of archetype opens the door for clients to know themselves in a new way.

Every skilled horse person knows that horses are sensitive to the things that we imagine and the pictures, even subconscious imprints, in our mind's feeling eye. When our therapy horse Frieda picks a client, we know she will be tapping that person's inner royalty. Queens do not consort with paupers. When Gem gravitates to a client on the basis of resonance, she is most likely sensing an activated inner child. In this way the herd incorporates and heals its members, horse or human.

Ask, Seek and Knock in practice   (A Key Five handout for adult clients)

What is intuition? When people work with horses, they notice that every moment is full of questions and inner judgments. Should I approach now? Is the horse playful, or angry, or afraid? Is the horse ready to come to me, are they inviting me to approach? Delicate questions with no right answer, and each moment is full of them. How can we know for sure?

And so we sense into our own body, looking for a "gut feeling" or an intuitive hunch. But even our own subtle impressions are full of mystery. Are these feelings my own, or the horse's?

There is an art to this process of feeling. We must grasp a hunch, and follow it as we wait for more clues. It's called validating our own reality. It may be a hunch about what to do next, or a guess about what the horse is feeling and thinking. We are in a land where there is no "right" or "wrong." There is always the measure of what we hope to create, and whether our actions and our reading of the situation serve that intention.

The feelings are so subtle, we must imagine into them to find their reality. You might ask, but if we are "only" imagining, then doesn't the horse become simply a canvas onto which we paint our fantasies? If we watch carefully, if we are open to the horse's feedback, and if we stay tuned in to our own subtle inner experience, more will be revealed as the interaction and relationship develop.

The challenge inherent in developing intuition is to see outer reality as clearly as possible, to discern in our inner experience not only threads of truth, but also threads of projection, wishful thinking, and denial of uncomfortable truths. At first, this level of self-honesty may feel very vulnerable, but it allows us to establish soul-to-soul contact that leads to richer, more positive relationships with horses and humans.

Use your keys consistently, and practice somatic awareness combined with observation of your outer situation. Illuminate your inner sensations by developing and training your imagination. The horse's responses will illuminate which information is valid and which may be products of your own imagination. Keep an open mind. Always let more be revealed.

> "SEEKING is the master emotion, and listening with the heart is wisdom.
> Seeking with a listening heart enables a Spirit-filled life."   ~David Young

Chapter Eight

The Sixth Key: The Successful Social Brain

"Social bonding in the mammalian brain probably goes hand-in-hand with the experience of loneliness, grief, and other feelings of social loss. To be alone and lonely ... are among the worst and most commonplace emotional pains humans must endure."

Jaak Panksepp

Affective Neuroscience: The Foundations of Human and Animal Emotions

THERAPEUTIC STRATEGY IN KEY SIX: THE (SUCCESSFUL) SOCIAL BRAIN

An African proverb says, it takes only one woman to bear a child, but it takes a village to raise it. Humans need community to thrive. Human relationships are incredibly complex—yet they are created from the same neural structures for social-emotional relating used by all of our mammalian ancestors. Relationships always entail sacrifice, and not all are healthy and beneficial. Human relationships are complex and stressful; the client's expanded window of tolerance will be helpful as he or she bridges EFPL learning to human relationships. Relationships will become more comfortable and rewarding as the client begins to grasp each of the Six Keys, and begins to put them into tentative practice.

Using Key Six, the therapist helps the client practice actions and choices that contribute to enduring and positive relationships—and helps the client compare and contrast horse and human relationships. The evidence of EFPL success will be healthier, more successful social relationships at all levels, from intimacy and parenting to friendships and community. Good relationships are a resilience factor that reliably results in symptom reduction, improved coping, and increased life satisfaction. The goal of HEAL EFPL remains an expanded social "tool kit" to help the client nurture a village of healthy human connections.

The chemistry of connection is a product of the complex, oxytocin-based nurturant circuits in the mammalian brain CARE circuits (Panksepp, 1998, p. 246). These most fundamental maternal bonds expand to other kinds of love, such as pair bonding, and other meaningful social and community bonds. The behavioral primes associated with the CARE circuit prepare mammals to protect, nurture and show affection, in all kinds of species-specific ways.

Mares with new foals can offer a crash course in early imprinting. The precocious foals are galloping alongside their mum within a day, along with getting licked, nuzzled *and* gently disciplined! Even in mature horses, we see evidence of a sophisticated limbic life: precise behaviors of caring and friendship that have roots in CARE circuits. An attitude of loving friendship and protection is shown by the head of one horse over the back of another (often the other horse may be lying down). Licking is a way of comforting other horses that are in pain, and is not uncommon behavior from the horse in EFPL sessions. Even the "bite on the butt" that drives a herd member further along, provides the security of structure in the herd—just like the parental ability to set boundaries in human families.

Since horses literally require care, training and handling from humans, EFPL is rich with opportunities for grooming, feeding and expressing care in myriad practical or sentimental ways. Activities that involve caring for the horse present a natural avenue into a client's experience of being cared for, particularly with child clients. Adult clients often view the tasks of horse care as a precious opportunity to experience their body as an instrument of connection and service to others, and also pleasurable in its strength and coordination.

The client's readiness to terminate therapy is often signaled by their degree of competence and confidence in natural human relationships. A key challenge is to anchor and generalize learning from EFPL and to create bridges to progress in the client's human relationships. During the culmination stage of therapy (typically characterized by emotional revision) the emphasis in the EFPL activities is on collaboration, trust and enjoyment; feelings of belonging, connection and accomplishment.

I've chosen, in this book, to consider mature pair bonding within the CARE circuits that prime the organism for attachment relationships. This oversimplifies a complex situation, because sexual behavior primes reside primarily in the LUST circuit. However, the many varieties of attachment all have roots in oxytocin-, opioid-, and prolactin-based neural systems. As Panksepp (1998, p. 246) says, "The nurturant circuits in the mother's brain and care-soliciting circuits in infants are closely intermeshed with those that control sexuality in the limbic areas of the brain ... males can also learn nurturing behaviors, and it is intriguing that sexual activity can strengthen anti-aggressive, caregiving substrates in the male brain."

The need for togetherness and social contact is not a value judgment, it's a biological fact. This need can be met in any number of healthy and soulful ways that look quite unique. It is important to stress the resilience and adaptability of the attachment systems. Even in the midst of trauma, attachments develop, primed by the need to survive. Attachments are shaped by survival, and healing happens when people shift their patterns to support thriving in the present, not just surviving based on past realities.

Overall, the reassurance of social care and mutual aid is built into the mammalian mind from the deepest recesses of our evolution and the earliest moments of our developing organism in the womb. Depression and anxiety are the inevitable consequences of an impoverished social environment and lack of social support, as shown in Figure 7.

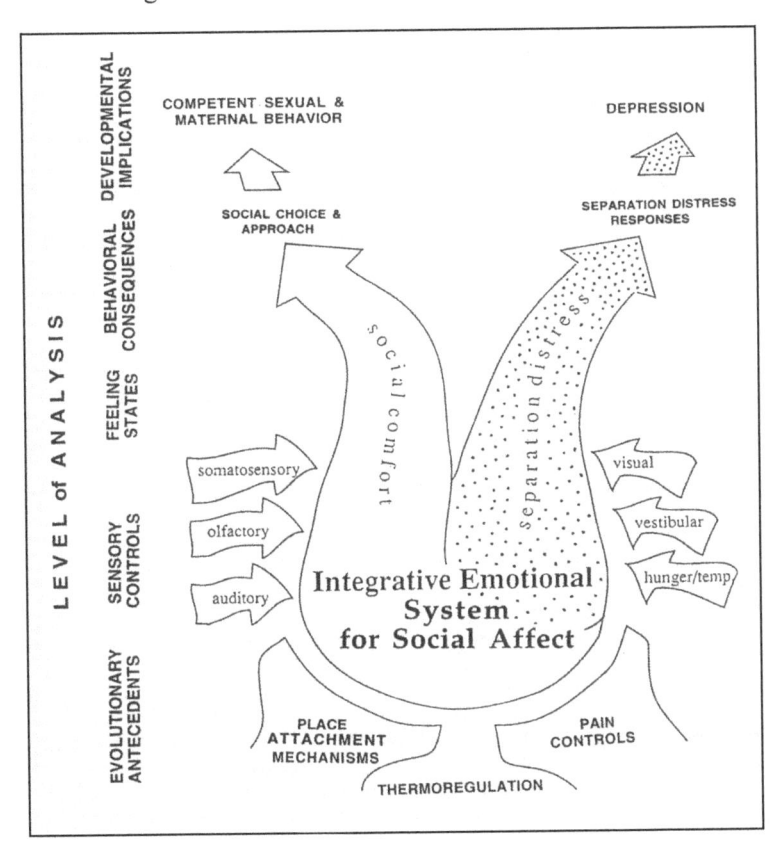

Figure 7. *Panksepp's Integrative Emotional System for Social Affect. CARE circuits are part of the most ancient architecture of the brain, emerging early in evolution and development from the fundamental capacities of pain controls, warmth, and place attachment, as shown in this schematic diagram.*

From *Affective Neuroscience*, 1998, p. 263. Used with author's permission.

A wide diversity of social configurations can *work; but isolation does* not *work.* Animals can readily fit into a human's limbic world. As Lewis et al. (2000, p. 98) state, "Somehow the attachment architecture is general enough that a human being and a dog can both fit within the realm of what each considers a valid partner … the two can engage in limbic regulation; they spend time near each other and miss each other; they read many of each other's emotional cues; each will find the presence of the other soothing and comforting; each will tune and regulate the physiology of the other. Limbic regulation is life sustaining." But we still need other humans as well. We will never shed our neural heritage as highly social mammals. The relationships that help us thrive include many levels of human social intimacy and assistance in getting one's needs met.

For many adults, marriage or domestic partnership, with or without children, provides the central structure to their limbic world. For those who remain single, it is possible to thrive on a good handful of close, authentic relationships that fulfill a range of emotional needs. Some people thrive on being at the center of communities, while others like a good portion of solitude. Some people really love to have animals as part of the community, while some people "don't really get" the animal thing. Understanding the deep mammalian need for attachments within our own species allows the clinician, by exploring Key Six with the client, to encourage the client to cultivate and evolve (and sometimes prune) their own *human* network of relationships.

TYPICAL EFPL ACTIVITIES FOR KEY SIX

The horse activities used to explore Key Six can be built around the many routines of caring for horses that are implicit in the horse environment. The client can be involved with grooming, feeding, keeping the barn tidy and safe for horses, and learning about them. These activities can emphasize a theme of love and mindfulness in action. These are activities that are best done in certain rhythms—seasonally, weekly or daily; and moment by moment body rhythms such as brushing and walking.

The increased familiarity with the horse that comes from caring activities helps to develop empathy in ways that are concrete and practical. A more realistic recognition of the horse as a separate being occurs, along with a greater depth of attachment that comes from investment in the relationship. These activities allow the horse to be a teacher of organization and sacrifice given willingly to support another being. The care of therapy horses should reflect these values.

From herd observation to grooming, handling and exercising the horses give a therapist and client myriad opportunities to explore the dynamics of caring relationships. The client and horse are building an interspecies working friendship; the therapist will find opportunities for the client to explore the relationship between caring and responsibility.

Throughout a client's course of therapy, activities such as grooming, and helping with feeding or medicating the horse build a habit of caring, and allow the client to experience the mutual pleasure of giving and receiving care. Many of the activities of caring for horses are rhythmic, physical, repetitive and grounding. If it is hands-on work with the horse then it also involves maintaining a limbic connection throughout.

When the client is in the completion stage of therapy, one of two things may happen. For some clients the horses will now assume less importance as the client has learned to trust the human therapist and is engaged in making conscious bridges to their important human relationships. For other clients, the relationship with the horse feels deep and very personal and there may be significant sadness in detaching. Clients often write poetry or use art to express their feelings for the horse. The therapist helps the client create and share transitional objects that will anchor the importance of this experience.

Transitions and passings in the therapy herd must be carefully handled. For some clients the horses become larger-than-life attachment figures. At HEAL, for many years we had a tall and distinguished thoroughbred named Galant. Galant had the knack of staying with people as an anchor, an inner representation of their experience at HEAL. When Galant died, our responsibilities included care for the emotional needs of our clients as well as the needs of our horse during a critical time. We are not meant to protect each other from grief, but to help one another through it.

The horses are beautiful models for forgiveness, with lots of tolerance for our mistakes. They give a lot, often sacrificing, without resentment. People are imperfect and may disappoint, and we have to risk possible rejection; just as horses will be horses and so sometimes they will shy out of fright and we may fall off. Clients have often been failed by critical early relationships—mother/father—or wounded by abuse and/or trauma. The situations are heart-breaking. Perhaps they have never been loved or accepted by others and cannot trust or be authentic within the family of origin. Based on the individual, therapy may take longer, go slower, be more intense, or require extra-sensitive approaches.

Regardless of the story, life still starts with connection and so the core principles do not change even though the details do. If the client has engaged and made a commitment to earlier foundational skills, they will be seeing the results in more meaningful relationships.

Community also matters for horses. As herd animals, they function best and feel most secure when they live with other horses. While fresh separation leads to the distress of the PANIC circuit, both horses and people become flat in affect—dare we call it depressed?—in isolation. As Panksepp points out, "Social bonding in the mammalian brain probably goes hand in hand with the experience of loneliness, grief, and other feelings of social loss." (1998, p. 263)

❧ EFPL HORSE ACTIVITY ❧
Grooming and Exploring Regulation

There are many different ways to set up a grooming activity depending on the client(s). If the client is an individual, a good way to start is with the horse haltered and ground tied (lead rope dropped to the ground, using the command "whoa"). When the client is a couple or a family dyad it is good to designate one as the horse holder while the other grooms, then switch roles. In some cases I might assist in holding the horse, but generally prefer that the client themselves create the structure that will influence the horse to stand still. It is best if we are in the sand arena rather than on grass, which would make things much more challenging!

A grooming kit containing rubber curry comb, stiff brush, soft brush, mane and tail brush or comb, and a hoof pick should be provided. Clients can also be encouraged to groom and scratch bare-handed, which promotes feeling even more and connection. Young clients may need a stool that can be easily moved to either side of the horse and is safe to stand on.

I have found it best to introduce this activity by talking with the client about mutual regulation, helping them to understand that they should soothe, not force, the horse into stillness. However, providing adequate structure that gives the horse clear and congruent communication can be regulating. On the other hand, if the horse is unable to stand still, directing them gently to move around can help in regaining the horse's attention. While the first task is encouraging the horse to stand, this is not necessarily a linear process.

When grooming commences, the horse will have some reactions and opinions about the grooming itself, expressing whether it is comfortable for them or not. In addition to the physical sensations, the horse will be responsive—in some cases even reactive—to the handler's autonomic state. In other words, if the client is breathing shallowly, if their heart rate increases or if their thoughts wander to a nearby worry—the horse will know and usually become restless. As the horse relaxes and stands still the client(s) will begin to feel successful and regulated too. The horse will begin to enjoy the grooming especially when sufficient structure is provided that it can't simply walk off, and the groomer is responsive enough to provide a pleasurable experience.

Facilitation should be minimal to avoid distracting from the limbic connection forming between humans and horses. In most cases the successful soothing of all parties will flow back and forth like a wave of good feelings, amplifying with each pass. The horse will send lots of signals of satisfaction and pleasure; the person or people involved will feel successful and appreciated by the horse's gestures, and humans and horse will feel both calmed and satisfied. In time the feeling will crest and begin to subside. At this point the horse will begin to shift more and sometimes be moved to explore things outside of the relationship circle.

Debriefing will help clients consciously retrace the steps that helped them regulate the horse and themselves along the way. It is very helpful to have clients put into words the rewarding feelings they got from the interaction, as it integrates sub-cortical with cortical, and right-brain with left-brain hemispheres.

✣ EFPL HORSE ACTIVITY ✣
Clients Help Horses Learn to Trust

It is not uncommon to have horses new to our herd, that may themselves have some unresolved history. Once the horse is in an environment of good limbic handling, habits such as being hard to catch or head shy should gradually disappear. Many behaviors that are called stable vices in horses—cribbing (chewing on wood) and weaving, for instance—are self soothing habits developed during a stressful time in the horse's life. The scientific term for this is *stereotypy*—an abnormal repetitive behavior often seen in captive animals and almost never seen in animals in their natural environments (Grandin, 2009, p. 14). Stereotypies are rewarding because of the endorphins released and can become so powerfully ingrained that a horse will crib, for instance, rather than grazing.

Evaluating the horse with difficult or unusual habits stemming from unresolved history is a job for the professional horse specialist who understands the type of horse needed for EFPL. Traumatic stress from environment or from training is sadly not uncommon in the horse population. At HEAL we do not rescue horses and we do not seek out individuals with stress-related habits, but over the years we've had opportunities to bring in mistrustful horses, dissociative horses, and horses with stereotypies. Within our calm and supportive environment such self-soothing behaviors are often mitigated—not erased, but eased. Chances are that the behavior will always have a place in that horse's stress management repertoire, but in our roles as community members we can do a lot to support the horse that is healing from stress. Our clients often find it powerful to be involved in this process.

One horse named Jilly, on loan to us from a friend, was a "weaver." She was a very gentle horse, submissive really, and she spent many unoccupied moments rocking back and forth, taking a step to one side back to the middle, and then to the other side and back. This could go on for hours. I will not forget the reaction of one client, "Lydia," who had recently started therapy for anxiety and panic. The first time that she saw Jilly rocking, as she so often did, Lydia gasped, "She looks just like me—that's what I do when I feel very afraid!" Lydia went on to do significant therapeutic work with Jilly, exploring many variations on themes of codependence and control. Lydia found that by calming herself, then exerting her presence in gentle ways, she could influence Jilly to stay present as well. These self soothing, protective and rewarding behaviors (stereotypies) can be influenced for the better, but once learned they are difficult to strictly control.

In the matter of working with the horse who displays stress regulation stereotypies or any potentially unsafe habit, the practitioner must consider the topic of liability and the highest service to the client. It is the clinician's responsibility to evaluate the horse for safety and the needs of the horse should never take priority over the needs of the client. Nevertheless, there are situations where needs are met synergistically—in nature this is more often than not the case.

Jilly worked with many clients and it was clear that only by keeping their own arousal down and their boundaries clear, could they help Jilly not weave so much. Some clients struggled with the feeling that Jilly was "suffering"—but really, she was not. Under a very small amount of stress Jilly would pick up her habit, a bit like an old woman hooking up her knitting. The activity soothed her, and she felt happy—but like an addict she missed out on real life.

Lydia noticed that certain other herd members were successful in keeping Jilly socially connected, which diminished her time spent in mindless weaving. Our other horse, Dixsi, would stand by Jilly, occasionally touching with her nose as if trying to get her attention. Dixsi's attention frequently drew Jilly back to grazing. But when it didn't, Dixsi would just stand by her.

A horse named Cloud entered our herd about two years ago. An older horse, Cloud was quite suspicious of humans. He could be difficult to approach and halter. Once "caught," his attitude toward humans at first was dismissive and sometimes a little defiant, in spite of being a well-trained riding horse. Cloud learned to trust person by person, clients included. Many of our clients had a role in Cloud's recovery. He was allowed to decline being caught—there were other herd members always willing step up (equine social learning!). We did some reward-based clicker training with Cloud, who began to enjoy learning and 'work' when it had this added element of precision and reward.

Cloud is a good example of a horse who was dissociative. The attitude that I first identified as "dismissive" became "positively not there" under a small amount of stress—usually the presence of cues that for him based on his past meant "here comes the pressure." In response, he was likely to pick up a trot or canter (at liberty, longeing or under saddle). Not only would he ignore any further demands, but we could tell he was truly dissociative because he no longer responded to the click. The click is like a reverse trigger—a trigger that means "you did the right thing and the reward is imminent." If the horse doesn't notice the click, he's not there!

It is moving, and often powerfully healing for the client to participate in the care of therapy animals, even helping in the barn with grooming, feeding and cleaning routines. However, care is warranted to model the same level of clarity and responsibility in relationship that we teach. The clinician should be proactive with policies and procedures that ensure clear boundaries and an emotionally safe environment. At HEAL, we encourage clients to transition to natural resources (a riding instructor, or volunteering at another center) if they wish to continue learning horsemanship and horse care after therapy ends.

◈ EFPL FACILITATION TOPIC ◈
Levels of Congruence

One of the most challenging things about EFPL in practice is that it requires of the practitioner an exceptionally high level of personal and emotional congruence. The most obvious aspect of this is that the horse will be carefully sensing all beings involved in the session, including yourself as the practitioner, your assistants and of course, any other horses involved. If the practitioner is suppressing emotion, the horse is likely to reflect or respond to that in some way. As the practitioner, it is best to disclose one's own emotions gracefully and succinctly to the client, modeling healthy boundaries in the process.

During EFPL sessions the client has many opportunities to notice consistency in care at all levels. It is important, therefore, to ensure that our actions speak as loudly as our words, both in and out of the formal session. For instance, when I put a saddle on the horse for an EFPL activity, how might I react if the horse turns toward me with bared teeth when I tighten the girth (or western cinch)? Do I act reflexively from my brainstem with a sense of threat? Do I set a boundary that protects myself? Is there a way in which I can influence the horse to be more comfortable with this activity—taking extra time with it, making sure that I breathe out a sense of assurance toward the horse as I gently snug the girth? If you hit the horse, your client will notice. If you allow the horse to violate your space, the client will notice. If you keep boundaries and create win-win solutions, the client will notice—and breathe more easily.

Across-the-board, an EFPL clinician will be well served to remember Temple Grandin's adage when it comes to keeping mammals happy, and apply this principle within their own equine domain. Soothe your horses and manage them in ways that minimize heightened arousal of intense FEAR, PANIC and RAGE. It is helpful to use productive training strategies to stretch their window of tolerance for challenging situations. Create and use the opportunities to share with horses all of the PLAY and SEEKING time will allow.

As stated in *A General Theory of Love* (Lewis et al., 2000, p. 208), "Because relationships are mutual, partners share a single fate: no action benefits one and harms the other. [Partners] ... share in one process, one dance, one story. Whatever improves that one benefits both; whatever detracts hurts and weakens both lives."

MORE ABOUT KEY SIX: THE SOCIAL BRAIN

Emotions that have their primary and secondary roots in the CARE circuits produce the warm feelings we humans call acceptance, nurturance and love. Biologically these good feelings have their basis in the endogenous opiates and oxytocin-based hormonal systems. These brain systems exert powerful effects on our physical well-being and health.

Perhaps it is not surprising then that the loss of important relationships creates painful feelings of loneliness, bereavement or abandonment. In fact, the limbic region of the brain has more receptor sites for endogenous opiates than any other brain area (Lewis et al., p. 94). Panksepp has outlined the surprising similarities between opiate dependence, and the key features of social attachment loss (1998, p. 255). This helps us recognize that grieving is very real and physical withdrawal. Therefore, it is extremely important how the therapist handles the termination/completion of therapy and issues of the death, serious illness or sale of a therapy horse. Transitional objects can be used very effectively such as pictures of the client with the horse, or a lock of hair from the horse's mane.

KEY SIX Vignette
Linda—Individual therapy, culmination stage

Linda came for therapy approximately twice a month for about two years. By the latter part of this time I could often allow her to arrive early, and groom Cloud on her own. This was soothing and regulating for Linda, activating the CARE circuits that were so much a topic of her therapy. Her circle of social connections slowly grew, including some 'friendship' dating with clear boundaries. "A HEAL Personal Growth workshop is coming up," I offered one day. "I thought you might be interested."

"Oh. No," Linda quickly insisted. Despite the negative response I noted her suppressed smile and flushed cheeks. Positive limbic signals. I waited. "I was afraid you'd say I should go," Linda continued when I remained silent. She took a deep breath, "And I really want to."

Coming to a workshop is a fairly typical Key Six activity for a client who has worked hard to overcome mistrust of people (or, a pattern of trusting the wrong people). For Linda there were many facets to vulnerability—remaining open with strangers, not rushing to judge herself, and feeling intensely critical of others (which she now recognized as projection). When she arrived for the first morning of the workshop, she told me later, she "almost bolted." But you know what? Linda had a rich time. She was able to let herself be revealed in the EFPL activities and in the sharing of group process. Time proved that two enduring friendships with other attendees, sprouted from this workshop. Natural relationships were replacing Linda's need for therapy, a sign that it was time to plan for termination.

Tina, PTSD group treatment 7th session

In our final group sessions each girl was given an opportunity to dance with her horse at liberty in the round pen. It's not a performance per se, though we do play music. It's an act of spontaneous co-creation with the horse as partner. Beau added a move of his own. Previously trained to bow on command, each time Tina turned toward Beau, he bowed! Tina did not know he could do this, nor had she presented a cue; Beau was offering simply to please her! Tina could do nothing but bow back. Her peers could not restrain their delighted admiration at the end, causing Tina to break into a wide grin that she could not hide. The group had become a significant source of safe support for each girl during the summer break from school.

In such brief interventions, especially with adolescent clients, we hope that the EFPL will serve as one experience that can confer greater resilience in a life already taxed by trauma, a life that may lack other social support and resources as well. In one short summer Tina evidenced a change that showed in her bearing and posture; a change that even a horse will bow to.

The goal is a capacity for healthy interdependence that suits the person's needs. Not everyone is a joiner, a herd leader, or a central figure in community. Whether it is five people or twenty-five people, our ability to feel successful in life's important relationships is central to psychological well-being. And it is also the stuff of miracles. One client remarked, "I started out in this process thinking I would finally find out what is wrong with me. As it turns out I found out what is right with me."

The limbic connection enables amazing leaps of intelligence, in people and in animals too. A wonderful modern-day example is the horse Lukas, owned by Karen Murdock (see references). Once labeled a rogue and a throw-away, Lukas found in Karen a person who understood him, someone he could trust. Lukas has since become a popular performer to demonstrate the power of positive training and the role of love and connection in learning. Lukas has attracted world-wide attention and is certified in the *Guinness Book of World Records* for "most numbers correctly identified in one minute" (source www.playingwithlukas.com).

Another example also involves a horse called "Jim" because as a colt he was so sickly he resembled the town drunk. Jim was "trained by kindness" by his owner Dr. William Key, a post-Civil War black man who nursed the sickly foal to wellness, then developed Jim to become the "Smartest Horse in the World," first mascot of the humane movement (Rivas, 2005).

And it is the same with people, isn't it? We all know stories of kids in the "slow class" who blossomed at an amazing rate in the hands of an emotionally attuned mentor. Healthy emotional experiences, even between a person and a horse, amplify learning, seeking and self-confidence. For many of our clients, the result is magic.

Chapter Nine

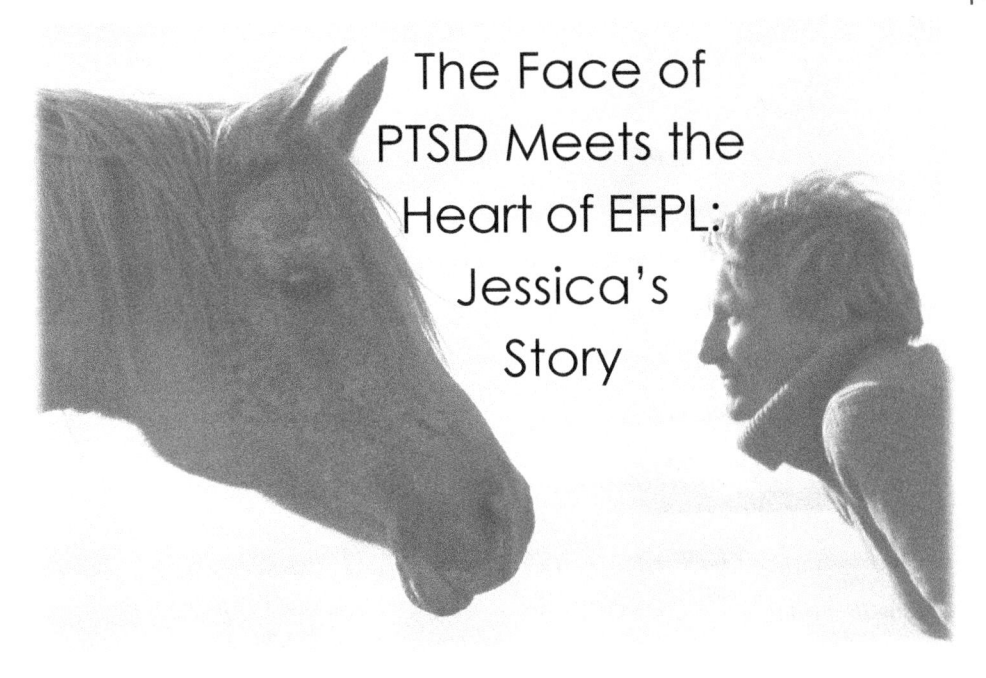

The Face of PTSD Meets the Heart of EFPL: Jessica's Story

"There are two kinds of old stories in a person's life: those worth cherishing and repeating, over and over, and the ones that are painful to remember. If they are continually repeated, traumatic stories have a way of defining a person, binding them to an identity best left in the past."

Jessica

JESSICA'S STORY AS TOLD TO THE AUTHORS

I used to throw up my old stories, literally and figuratively. First, in the body-hating condition of an eating disorder—anorexia and bulimia—then in personal relationships when I felt compelled to dump painful memories and traumatic details (my "stuff") on those close to me. I thought connection and intimacy would happen naturally by sharing my background like that. It doesn't. People are tempted to compare and contrast experiences and judge or label a person because of the terrible things that happened to them. For those reasons, and others, I am choosing not to disclose the nature of the abuse that drove me to eventually seek treatment at Remuda Ranch, an inpatient program for eating and anxiety disorders in Wickenburg, AZ. After various assessments and work with a therapist it was concluded that I suffered from Post Traumatic Stress Disorder.

Your own trauma may be greater or lesser than mine. It doesn't really matter. What matters is the choice to embrace a process that enables you to get out of the cycle of PTSD and write a new chapter in the story of your life. What follows are some snap shots of my own process and how a few horses helped carry me to the other side of trauma. Horses don't care about old stories; they don't feel sorry for you or assign labels like "sick/needy/depressed." You can simply be yourself with a horse; they seem to look for the strength inside, strength you didn't even know you had.

I didn't grow up with horses, but they were part of what drew me to the program at Remuda Ranch. The program included twice weekly therapy that included horses. I had a lot of anxiety in those days so talking about things could be difficult. At Remuda I developed a special friendship with a horse named Larimee. Larimee helped me feel quiet inside. I could trust him in a way I hadn't been able to trust the people in my life at that time. It's been ten years since I've seen Larimee, but he still lives in my heart and I remember the feeling of being with him. The word remuda is Spanish for a group of horses used to give rest and a fresh start for the journey ahead. This is what equine therapy has helped give me: a fresh start.

The experiences with horses during inpatient treatment were significant enough to encourage me to take horseback riding lessons when I returned to the Pacific Northwest. I made a new friend in elderly "Bucky," a buckskin gelding with a youthful zest for life and playful energy. From Bucky I learned more about horsemanship and the importance of personal boundaries. When I protected my boundaries from Bucky's pushy behavior he didn't abandon me, our relationship got better. Bucky also seemed to react to my emotions. When I held back tears or other strong feelings Bucky would push his nose into my belly as if he felt that energy. This made me curious and I wanted to learn more about how horses connected to people this way.

With the exception of a feeling called "fat," I didn't even know I had emotions for a large part of my life. My physical body and internal self existed in separate locales. I talked about my body as if it were an entity I only vaguely recognized. When negative feelings and fear took over I completely shut down in a way therapists call dissociation. Dissociation helps you cope when feelings and sensations inside become overwhelming. Through inpatient treatment at Remuda and ongoing therapy afterward, I was able to break free of the cycle of PTSD and the life-threatening conditions of anorexia and bulimia.

While taking lessons with Bucky, I heard about HEAL and was drawn to investigate the workshops offered there. One was called Overcoming Anxiety and Fear. I'd lived most my life in fear: fear of judgment, abandonment, and connection. Fear of someone hurting me. While I was busy working on a new life story, I still felt a disconnect between my mind and body and thought it was worth exploring.

I arrived at HEAL in the summer of 2009 with no expectations, just a skeptical sort of curiosity. The natural setting did its usual magic: I breathe easier around horses. The workshop began with an exercise called Meet and Greet. We practiced listening to our bodies through mind/body awareness techniques. I practiced something called a body scan. The truth that emotions manifest themselves in the body as various sensations was a completely new idea for me. Because my mind and body were always separate, it seemed as if the place *of being overwhelmed just happened and there was nothing I could do about it.*

As the workshop progressed my anxiety began to rise. Regardless of the wonderfully natural setting, I found it hard to relax around Leigh. The presence of a therapist triggered something inside. Therapy is healing, but it is also challenging and stressful. Some of the worst stress came when I saw a male therapist for the first time six years after Remuda Ranch. It was terrifying to imagine being alone in a room with a man. I almost threw up the night before our first appointment. But, ultimately, that time of vulnerability strengthened me and I cherish the work we did. Now, years later, my old self was being triggered again by the environment at HEAL.

There's always some fear and pressure involved with a new therapist, almost a kind of performance anxiety. I thought Leigh probably saw me with all the old labels glowing like a neon sign: Messed Up, Broken, and Sick. I took a deep breath and asked to speak to her.

"I'm having a reaction to you," I said. "I feel like I am getting stuck in that role of being screwed up. I have some issues, still, but I am not the same person I was. I guess I need to know how you have perceived me so far."

We'd been working on boundary exercises with the horses. To be honest, I wasn't prepared to have the issues I still had with boundaries revealed in a group setting so obviously and quickly. That's the thing about horses; you can't filter what you share. It just happens and sometimes the deep emotions feel kind of raw. In an office it usually takes longer to feel comfortable revealing certain things to a therapist—I'm always afraid they'll run away screaming! I guess I'm hypersensitive to other people and what they think of me. This sensitivity helps me read horses, but sometimes it makes me more anxious around people. I'd shared some of my abuse and eating disorder history with Leigh and now I needed to know she hadn't labeled me with it permanently. My anxiety rose as I waited for her answer. Somehow I trusted she'd find a way to kindly tell me if she thought I looked like damaged goods.

"I have sensed you have a story," Leigh said, "but you aren't afraid to deal with your issues. I respect that."

Shame is a powerful thing that can shut a person down completely. It keeps many trauma survivors like me in silence and agony. We talked about wounded stories a little then, and how each of us can help others heal when we walk through a difficult place. At that moment I didn't feel ashamed of my past.

A list of words to describe the way I once saw myself would include these: needy, messed up, immature, high maintenance, over-sensitive, sick. Despite the worthwhile work I'd done on myself to that point, I didn't think I had much strength or leadership. That's why it was pretty funny that the horse I practiced with in the Reflective Round Pen exercise was Frieda, the boss mare of the HEAL herd. A regal bay "Queen," Frieda doesn't do anything she doesn't want to and is completely confident and secure. At first Frieda seemed to have no need for me. She ignored me completely. I must admit the Reflective Round Pen exercise struck me as sorta hokey. I mean, it's pretty subjective; what's to prevent a person from saying or claiming whatever they want?

Despite my skepticisms, I really wanted something deep and emotional to happen in this exercise. When nothing happened I felt frustrated—I couldn't even engage a horse! When Leigh came over she asked a simple question: What would it look like if you were the queen, you were the leader?

When I get frustrated or overwhelmed it's tempting to just quit, make the feeling go away. But I had an idea and decided to persevere. I approached Frieda, gently touched the underside of her jaw and said, "Let's go this way." To my surprise, she followed me willingly. It was then I realized I am scared of being in charge, of having power and abilities. In my family, I didn't have a lot of power or strength. The experience of leading a leader like Frieda empowered me in a way I'd never imagined.

It was when I stepped into my strength that I experienced connection with Frieda. This was a light bulb moment for me. I'd never realized I carried an unconscious belief that if I was strong it would take something away from somebody else, like I had to sacrifice myself in a relationship if I wanted to avoid abandonment. Frieda lost nothing by me being strong—and I wasn't rejected! That one thing is a memory I still turn to; it nurtures who I am becoming.

The best part of the workshop came at the very last day when it was time to "dance" with a horse in an active culminating exercise. I let myself become completely hokey and closed my eyes as I thought about which horse to choose. I wanted to just let go and forget about anxious fears.

The horse I felt drawn to stood quietly in a stall. Nobody had worked with him all weekend so I knew nothing about him. The biggest horse at the ranch, Galant literally towered over me. I decided to let my strength match his. Leigh put on some music and I moved back and forth with Galant, slowly at first. He watched me carefully and we began moving faster. He started trotting and then cantering around me. He kicked up his heels in pure pleasure as I felt my heart swell. In that moment I felt no fear. Maybe it sounds weird, but it felt like Galant matched everything I felt inside—joy, confidence, freedom of spirit. It is hard to explain in words, but the feeling of that day still gives me strength and pleasure when I remember it. I looked up the word 'gallant' later. It means: Noble in bearing or spirit; brave; high spirited; courageous; heroic; bravery on extraordinary occasions in a spirit of adventure.

At the end of the workshop, the other participants gave me a new list of words to define myself with. They included "bold" and "dynamic." My favorite description was "gentle strength." I cried then and shared some vulnerable moments. Being vulnerable can be good I've learned, it doesn't necessarily mean something bad will happen. No more "needy," no more "messed up." Those words do not define me anymore. Horses invited the healthy places inside me to blossom and that's what everyone saw at the end of that workshop. Amazing.

I did more work with the horses at HEAL after that and had more light bulb moments. Horses aren't people, but they did become my friends and let me practice all the things I learned in therapy about being connected in a safe way. Those experiences still influence me and the life I'm living now.

Today I'm finishing up a psychology degree. I hope to work with children in the future and my dream is that it will include horses somehow, some way. Horses have a way of showing people where they are strong, not defining them by the trauma of an old story. The revelations I had in the company of horses remind me of a favorite passage from Marianne Williamson's book A Return to Love: Reflections on the Course in Miracles, (Harper Collins 1992, pages 190-191).

> *Our deepest fear is not that we are inadequate. Our deepest fear is that we are powerful beyond measure. It is our light, not our darkness that most frightens us. We ask ourselves, Who am I to be brilliant, gorgeous, talented, fabulous? Actually, who are you not to be? You are a child of God. Your playing small does not serve the world. There is nothing enlightened about shrinking so that other people won't feel insecure around you. We are all meant to shine, as children do. We were born to make manifest the glory of God that is within us. It's not just in some of us; it's in everyone. And as we let our own light shine, we unconsciously give other people permission to do the same. As we are liberated from our own fear, our presence automatically liberates others.*

Chapter Ten

The Listening Heart

*"If SEEKING is the master emotion, and listening with the heart is wisdom ...
Seeking with a listening heart enables a Spirit-filled life."*

David Young

Perhaps it is no accident that the word we use for a lively, proud horse is "spirited." Spirited horses can be a challenge even for experienced equestrians, who must know how to flow with them, and be strategic in trying to direct them. It takes a light hand, and a wise one.

Spirited is a word we might use to describe Equine-Facilitated Psychotherapy and Learning (EFPL) itself. The introduction of horses to the therapy relationship brings with it a significant element of unpredictability and vulnerability, along with a huge wealth of resilience and grace. It's a bit like creating a calculated opening for divine synchronicity to show up in your session. It's a bit intimidating at first. But session by session I have discovered that, as my friend, equine artist Kim McElroy, says, "Nothing never happens."

Lavender (2006, p. 53) says, "The horse's agenda is to join.... Could it be that the horse is getting needs met as well? ... Symbiosis is the order of the day rather than one or the other functioning in isolation." It is a symbiosis that will also include the therapist and team members along with the client. For horses, the joining is inclusive rather than exclusive. No matter our position—at the center or on the fringe—we are always part of the herd. Belonging is a given.

While the HEAL Model is based in what is natural for mammals, that does not mean that it is simple, especially when working with a clinical population. Successful implementation of the HEAL Model calls for a variety of developed skills in the therapist and other team members. These are not strictly clinical skills or theoretical skills. Consider this: two humans enter a horse's pen; no labels tell the horse which person is "therapist" or "client." The horse will sense in each their needs, their defenses and the amount of nervous system arousal, equally. It is therefore imperative that the therapist and other members of the team be congruent, present, attuned and responsive. Where the office based therapist may find it relatively easy to compartmentalize "their own stuff"—in the horse arena this is virtually impossible.

In EFPL, the clinician is arguably at greater risk than ever of pushing an agenda or belief system of their own because we work with a partner who literally can't contradict us using words. Many of us are 'horse lovers' with strong feelings for the care and comfort of our equine colleagues. For instance, I consulted with one EFPL practitioner who believed it "unfair" to have "more than one client at a time with the horse" (this was not riding work, only ground work). When I questioned this belief she elaborated that it could be "confusing" and "too much pressure" for the horse to sense and respond to more than one client at a time. We discussed at length the fact that for horses, *the natural condition is to be attuned to several other beings at once*, which helped her keep an open mind. As this practitioner gained experience, she also learned that not only was it not harmful to the horse—it was a virtual necessity for clients such as married couples or parent-child dyads to be able to work with the horse together. To me, such an attitude would constitute an unnecessary attitude of protectionism toward the horse—likely the practitioner's projection onto the horse.

Following limbic processes in the client *and* the horse as co-therapist, requires the practitioner to "navigate by feeling" and facilitate the client in doing the same. It is often necessary to follow the horse and trust the horse, whose limbic voice will only be revealed when we are able to wait, allow and watch for it. This may feel very vulnerable to therapists used to more structured interventions.

An EFPL practice will include many unexpected things which happen in a horse facility setting, which would not happen in office therapy: a horseshoer shows up at the wrong time for an appointment, or an unexpected health problem necessitates veterinary intervention— situations which can quickly become emotional for some clients. In these "real life" situations, as well as interactions with the horse, the client can observe and sense the therapist (and other team members) 'in action,' navigating boundaries and flowing with the unexpected.

In fact, there *is* vulnerability here. For any of us humans, living in authentic, dynamic discourse with our own feelings will change us. As therapists, we are committed to helping others achieve this discourse with themselves, including the courage to make difficult changes in the service of developing a truer self. We might ask ourselves: are we really living our own journeys? It is my experience, after a decade of immersion in EFPL, that the preparation and establishment of an EFPL practice will be as transformative for the practitioner as it is for the designated clients. Likely the horses would laugh off such labels (as "client" and "therapist") as mere human "abstractification!" (Grandin, 2005, p. 27)

EFPL practitioners who are just starting often consider EFPL in terms of various traditional counseling and psychotherapy models—another abstraction! Suffice to say the therapist must embody an integration of somatic, cognitive and limbic (attachment) skills, as well as openness to various pathways of spiritual and intuitive knowing that the client might experience. The horse is nature. The approach must be 'bio-neuro-psycho-social-spiritual', with room to spare! As well, it must be grounded in sound assessment of each client's treatment needs. We are required to be responsible stewards on many levels.

The HEAL Model requires the practitioner to follow and facilitate the client's subtle signs of arousal or avoidance. In short the therapist should be conversant in both bottom-up (somatic) and top down (cognitive) therapeutic methods. It is also helpful to have some familiarity with experiential process work or Gestalt psychotherapy (or similar models).

Perhaps the biggest conceptual challenge is the understanding of the limbic world of both client and the horse, recognizing in subtle everyday behaviors the concerns of the limbic brain: Who can I count on? Who do I belong with? What's my relationship to you? Do you notice where you end and I begin? Is this relationship safe? Who do I need to look out for, and why? Resolution of these limbic questions for client and horse will lead to satisfaction and clarity in the human-horse relationship. Limbic understanding of the horse is probably the invisible quality referred to in the horse world as "feel."

Because the HEAL Model focuses on a working limbic bond with the horse, safety for the human-horse interactions (adequate but not overprotective) is built in. The model focuses on a bond where horse and human look for, and look out for, each other. This is a practical bond of energy and attention. It allows for subjectivity and intensely personal experiences of meaning while encouraging the reality testing that is a function of healthy ego strength.

The director of the public mental health agency, Cascade Mental Health Care (Chehalis, WA), which contracts with HEAL for PTSD groups, has called HEAL EFPL "cutting edge technology for mental health." (S. Killilay, personal communication, April 19, 2010). This publicly funded agency is mandated to "evidence-based" mental health practices. On the strength of our pilot study, ongoing research and the science behind our model, we have continued to serve this agency for four years. The HEAL Model represents a safe and clinically reliable EFPL Model for use with PTSD and other mental health disorders.

AFTERWORD

The Remuda

Spring 2012

My mother's birthday falls in April. Since her death in 1988, my 180 year, the Easter season has been an especially emotional time. I choose to remember the gift of her living, rather than the despair in which she ended her life. For me, this season of life after death, new growth, and fresh beginnings taps into a deep well of grief for a bright woman who died too soon. It seems no coincidence that as I wrap up this book with the theme of Remuda—A Fresh Start—April is dawning and another Easter of remembrance—and grieving—is around the corner.

It's amazing the places that God will lead a willing spirit. It was a horse that first pointed me toward the path to wholeness; God knew the manner in which I would be able to embrace certain mysteries and begin to trust unseen process. As a therapist, I know that true healing requires forgiveness. It is one of the primary goals of psychotherapy and a critical task for Key Six, the Home Run Key.

To achieve a fresh start, I'm no different than the clients that arrive at the HEAL Ranch—I must take responsibility for my emotions and make a choice to forgive the pain I have felt in those important relationships. Thus continues a journey that includes a feeling awareness, cognitive understanding, and conscious choices, woven together with mysterious grace. The process is equal parts spiritual and psychological.

This knowing creates a new chapter in my personal evolution. Hooray for brain plasticity and the possibility for fresh beginnings! The past may contain shadows, but we can always choose to head for the light; we can choose to forgive the times other people's histories have collided with our own and left us wounded. We can treat each other gently and remember we are all children of God, however we understand or name the life-giving energy.

As my friend and HEAL collaborator Kathleen Barry Ingram has said, the spirit wants to thrive, not merely survive. Functioning relationships—the ability to bond, connect and live effectively with others—is a foundation of a successful life. To move toward this goal many clients need relational experiences that help them heal—new experiences that create new understandings and practical ways to live a new story about relationships. For many of them the use of horses is a highly effective approach to this journey of the soul.

Throughout this book I have presented some of the latest understanding, practice, and science behind the effectiveness of employing horses in mental health and relationship therapy with a licensed provider. Licensed mental health therapists may be Social Workers, Psychologists, Counselors, and Marriage and Family Therapists. Licensed therapists are mental health care providers trained in the assessment and treatment of mental disorders and obligated to maintain current competence in the mental health field. Therapists from these diverse categories may employ EFPL within their practice in ways that fit the client and serve individual therapeutic goals. My hope is that EFPL will be embraced as a viable, professionally defensible modality for remediating mental illness, treating psychological distress, and healing the lingering effects of traumatic experience.

The high cost of horse care and the necessity of providing an appropriate treatment setting for EFPL pose very practical challenges for the qualified therapist. While a dog can be brought to the office, in EFPL the client must be brought to the horse. Additionally, the farm setting must provide the privacy, and physical and emotional safety that intensive mental health therapy requires. Research can substantiate the significant added value that EFPL contributes to the course of therapy, justifying the extra expense.

Additionally, research will help us determine which specific models of EFPL are most appropriate for diverse client populations. Accordingly, this book describes HEAL-sponsored clinical research built around our own client specialty: complex PTSD that leaves survivors with significant deficits in relational ability, often severe enough that even their ability to engage effectively in therapy is affected.

Science has proven the brain and body are imprinted by our life experiences, for better or worse. Our brains can only change and allow us to move out of negative patterns through experience, not simply acquiring cognitive knowledge. To this end, horses serve as a sophisticated means to engage a client in a real life relationship that leaves positive neural pathways of learning, pathways that can be returned to and strengthened. They fill a missing link in the practice of psychotherapy, especially for clients who can't trust anyone wearing a "human costume." The unassuming and forgiving partner wearing the "horse costume" allows imperfect human beings to practice and assimilate new, transferable skills.

For clients with damaged relational templates, the presence of a horse creates an emotionally safe place for treatment, and the horse becomes an engaging co-facilitator and support. Jessica's story helps us understand the shame and fear of judgment that often block effective treatment and recovery. As she discovered, fears are soothed and courage inspired by a sensitive and discerning silent witness. Horses, prey animals themselves, seem to sense the vulnerability of the human soul that often dwells in secret places and comes forward only when it feels safe. Moreover, by example they encourage forgiveness, which remains a central theme of effective therapy.

Many pioneers have gone before me and there is much work yet to do in a field often clothed in mystery or, at the very least, considered alternative. My deepest desire is that professional therapists, counselors and health care funders, as well as clients, will consider the usefulness of employing horses in mental health and relationship therapies. Throughout millennia, the horse has generously sacrificed itself to human use. Regardless of a decline in the need for horses as beasts of burden, the horse remains an object of grace, beauty, and profound inspiration that is also earthy and intimately accessible. The horse continues to prove itself a worthy and willing partner to the human heart.

APPENDIX A

HEAL–Sponsored Research

From Shambo, Seely and Vonderfecht, 2010. A Pilot Study on Equine-Facilitated Psychotherapy for Trauma-Related Disorders (Reprinted with permission from the authors.)

EFPL falls within a broad category of interventions known as animal-assisted therapies (AAT). A broad overview of AAT's theoretical foundations and practice considerations is provided by the *Handbook on Animal Assisted Therapy* (Fine, Ed., 2000). The manual notes that horses require a specialized site and pose greater safety and liability risks than smaller animals; but also offer " … a peak experience, perhaps unmatched by any other" (Hart, 2000, p. 94).

In EFPL horses are employed to treat emotional and behavioral disorders, usually as part of, or adjunct to, an overall treatment approach. EFPL emphasizes equine emotional responsiveness and capacity for complex social bonding (which includes humans). In EFPL, the horse is a sentient partner whose feelings and needs must be considered both on the ground and in the saddle, a fact underscored by their size and power. Horses are similar to humans in that they live in bonded social groups (herds), have defined roles within the herd and distinct personalities, attitudes, and moods, providing apt parallels for human social experience.

In two decades since its emergence, EFPL has been explored in popular books on the topic (Kohanov, 2001, 2003; McCormick & McCormick, 1997; Webb, 2002). Kohanov's works cite current literature from the fields of psychology and neuroscience to support her theory that horses are exceedingly sensitive to affective incongruence in humans. Kohanov asserts that working with horses can help trauma survivors understand the links between soma and psyche, learn to self-regulate affect and arousal, and modulate dissociative states (Kohanov, 2001).

The largest studies to date of EFPL's efficacy have focused on children. Treatment with EFPL improved scores on the Children's Global Assessment Functioning (GAF) in 63 children exposed to domestic violence (Schultz, Remick-Barlow & Robbins, 2007). Significant gains in GAF scores were correlated with the number of sessions (up to 19 in this study); age (younger children showing greatest gains); and personal experience of abuse or neglect (those with direct experience of abuse/neglect showing greatest improvement). Trotter (2006) measured frequency of negative and positive behaviors in elementary and middle school students using the Behavioral Assessment System for Children (BASC). The 140 students, "at risk for academic or social failure," were assigned to either EFPL group counseling sessions or a school-based guidance group. Students in the EFPL groups showed statistically significant improvement in a wider range of behavior areas compared to the school-based curriculum.

Evidence of EFPL's effectiveness in adult populations is difficult to find. One of the earliest articles on EFPL described the author's experience introducing riding to selected adult patients within the course of outpatient therapy (Tyler, 1994). In case vignettes, the author describes how trail riding with the client in some sessions resulted in increased disclosure of sensitive material, decrease in dissociative symptoms, and calmer affect for particular clients, positively influencing the course of treatment.

Two other small qualitative studies reported on the effect of weekly riding lessons for adults with long-standing psychiatric disability (non-specific as to diagnosis), provided as an adjunct to their regular treatment (Bizub, Joy & Davidson, 2003; Burgon, 2003). In both studies, the riding lessons were provided by staff at a therapeutic riding center, rather than facilitated by the therapist, and results were taken from client self-reports. The most frequently noted effects in both studies were increased self-confidence, ability to overcome fears, and enjoyment of the riding activity itself.

COMPLEX PTSD AS AN OPERATIONAL CONSTRUCT

Some of this literature suggests that EFPL is an intervention uniquely suited to ameliorating the effects of trauma stemming from interpersonal violence (Kohanov, 2001, 2003; Schultz et al., 2007; Tyler, 1994). The effects of this type of trauma are variable and multi-faceted, depending on the nature of the trauma, its duration and the developmental stage at which the trauma occurred. Responses occur across a spectrum of existing diagnostic categories, leading researchers to call for more nuanced and inclusive guidelines to diagnose PTSD in its more complex presentations (van der Kolk & Courtois, 2005; Roth, Newman, Pelcovitz, van der Kolk & Mandel, 1997).

For purposes of this study, the authors elected to use the more general conceptualization of "complex PTSD," originally proposed by Herman (1997). Complex PTSD is an operational construct that includes "... disorders of affect regulation, dissociation, chronic characterological changes in the area of self-concept, alterations in interpersonal relationships, and somatization" (McLean, 2004). This allowed us to consider potential candidates across diagnostic categories if a history of interpersonal trauma was present and when current treatment was failing to adequately restore psychological and interpersonal functioning.

Aside from diagnosing, the nature of complex PTSD makes for treatment challenges. Survivors have difficulty engaging in therapeutic alliance and experience shifting constellations of somatic, affective and behavioral symptoms (Herman, 1997; Linehan, 1993). Dissociative symptoms may be underreported and highly problematic for persons with complex PTSD (van der Hart, Nijenhuis, & Steele, 2005). Deficits in self-regulation of emotional-somatic response leave survivors extremely stress-vulnerable—while they function well in some circumstances, they can become quickly symptomatic in others (Linehan, 1993). Interestingly, this type of affective 'unreliability' can be seen in horses, who are exquisitely sensitive to context and to the subtle energies of those in their environment (Kohanov, 2003).

The authors formulated this research question: Would brief treatment with EFPL result in measurable, lasting change for women whose history of interpersonal trauma complicated their recovery from Axis I or II disorders? To answer this question, the authors developed a brief (10 sessions of 2 hours each) therapy group that combined EFPL with psychoeducation and mutual support via group process. A research director helped to develop a research protocol and performed statistical analysis of data. A local equestrian facility served as the site, and grant funding was secured to minimize costs to participants in order to study the treatment effects of EFPL, an unproven and relatively costly intervention.

Selection criteria were based on the DSM-IV diagnoses of PTSD, and/or Borderline Personality Disorder, as well as recommendations from the North American Riding for the Handicapped Association. Referrals were also based on the client's expressed interest in trying a therapy that included EFPL. Six individuals met the criteria for participation (N=6).[*] Study results are summarized in the slides on the following pages.

---

[*] Informed consent to participate in the study was obtained from all participants. Study design and implementation approved by Providence St. Peter Hospital Institutional Review Board.

Equine-Facilitated Psychotherapy for Trauma-Related Disorders

Pilot study of a 10-week EFP group for adult women

© 2008 Leigh Shambo MSW, LMHC
of Human-Equine Alliances for Learning

Authors and Special Thanks

Authors:

Leigh Shambo MSW, LMHC
Author & Group Facilitator
President and Lead Therapist, Human-Equine Alliances for Learning (HEAL)

Susan K. Seely RN, MN, ARNP
Group Co-Facilitator
Clinical Nurse Specialist in Adult Psychiatry and Mental Health

Heather R. Vonderfecht PhD
Research Director
Associate Professor of Social Work and Sociology
Walla Walla College School of Social Work

Special Thanks:
Providence St. Peter Hospital, Olympia, WA
Human-Equine Alliances for Learning (HEAL), Chehalis, WA
Sylvan Meadow Farm, Olympia, WA

What is Complex PTSD?

The damaging psychological effects of childhood physical and/or sexual abuse.

Characteristic Symptoms

    Flashbacks

    Nightmares

    Hypervigilance

    Emotional numbing

    Pervasive mood effects

    Transient to severe dissociation

    Dysfunctional & self-destructive personality patterns

- Many survivors have been diagnosed with personality disorders.
- Relational & developmental
- Recognized by experts although it has yet to be formalized in the DSM-IV.
- High co-occurrence with a number of adult psychiatric disorders on Axis I and II and with substance use disorders and somatic complaints.

Abstract

Purpose of this pilot study: To measure specific changes, and durability of changes, for adult women outpatients with complex PTSD when treated with EFP in a 10-week therapy group as an adjunct to treatment as usual.

- 6 adult women participated in a 10 week therapy group involving EFP combined with psychoeducation.

All participants met these criteria:

- Diagnosed w/ PTSD or Borderline PD
- Remained symptomatic with PTSD associated symptoms in spite of medication & outpatient counseling
- Still experienced symptoms severe enough to impair social and/or occupational functioning
- Had either refused or failed to benefit from traditional group therapy

- Measures for Depression, Anxiety, Dissociation, & overall treatment efficacy
- Standardized measures were taken at 4 points relative to treatment
  - Pre-treatment
  - Mid-treatment
  - Post-treatment
  - 4-moth post treatment
- Measures captured significant & enduring positive changes on these axes:
  - Depression & dissociative symptoms
  - Treatment effectiveness overall
- Change effect was dramatic and continued post-treatment as scores showed even more improvement at 4 month follow up

Hamilton Depression Scale – Mean Scores

- General clinical guide to the HAMD scores
  10-13: Mild
  14-17: Mild to moderate
  18+: Moderate to severe

- Looking at mean scores the trend is for the scores to go down consistently at each interval.

- Starting mean score of 27.5 indicates that on average these women were experiencing moderate to severe levels of depression.

- By the end their mean score of 12.17 places them in the low end of mild depression.

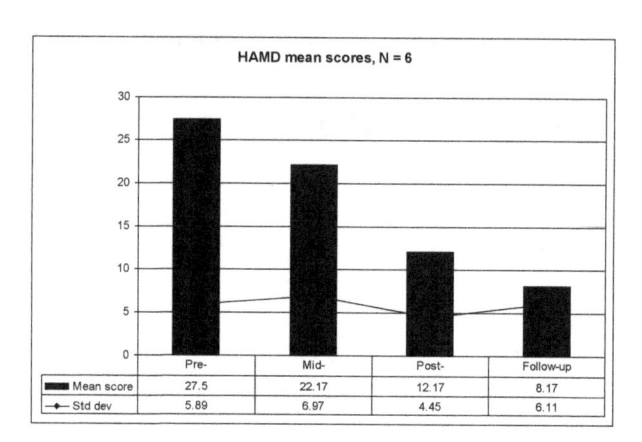

HAMD mean scores, N = 6

	Pre-	Mid-	Post-	Follow-up
Mean score	27.5	22.17	12.17	8.17
Std dev	5.89	6.97	4.45	6.11

- 4-month follow up mean score of 8.17 puts them in the normal, non-depressed range.

Beck Anxiety Inventory – Mean Scores

- General clinical guide rating
  0-21 – Very low
  22-35 – Moderate
  36+ – Severe

- Compares mid-treatment mean scores with post- and follow-up scores in paired T tests.

- Mid treatment: 42.5

- End of treatment: 33.5

- Follow-Up: 31.5

- Pre - post change: $t(5)=1.10$, $p=0.159$

- Mid - follow up change: $t(5)=1.95$, $p=0.054$

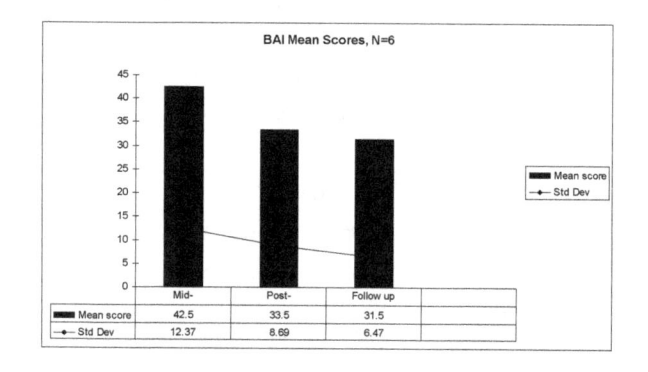

BAI Mean Scores, N=6

	Mid-	Post-	Follow up
Mean score	42.5	33.5	31.5
Std Dev	12.37	8.69	6.47

- Trend: lower level of anxiety symptoms but the data doesn't show statistical significance

- Mean scores indicate on avg. participants went from high anxiety to the higher end of moderate range

Dissociative Experiences Scale – Mean Scores

- Score above 30: Suggests likelihood of dissociation disorder
- Score above 45: possible Dissociative Identity Disorder
- Starting mean score: 22.71
- Mid treatment mean score: 16.70
- Post treatment mean score: 16.96
- Follow up mean score: 7.44
- Paired t-test pre to post: t(5)=1.29, p=0.13 (not significant)

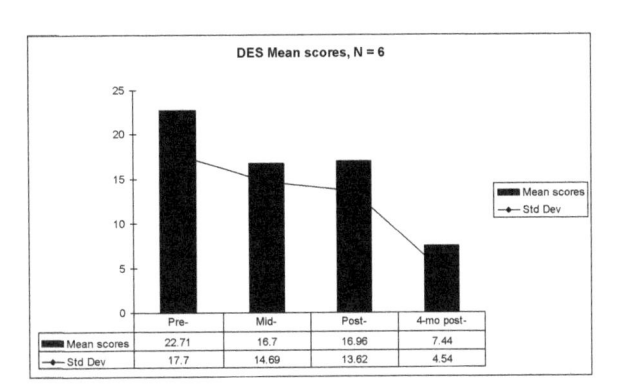

DES Mean scores, N = 6

	Pre-	Mid-	Post-	4-mo post-
Mean scores	22.71	16.7	16.96	7.44
Std Dev	17.7	14.69	13.62	4.54

- Paired t-test pre to follow up: t(5)=0.023 (very significant)

Interesting patterns in DES individual scores

- Two individuals entered treatment with very high scores indicating the likelihood of dissociative disorders as well as PTSD. By the follow up measure, all participants' individual scores are safely within the non-symptomatic range.

- Scrutiny of individual scores reveals the possibility of a negative correlation between dissociation and anxiety. It's possible that as dissociative symptoms decrease, anxiety will increase.

	DESPR	DESM	DESPO	DESFL
1	15.36	10.71	17.14	8.57
2	19.11	16.61	11.43	10.00
3	7.14	4.29	7.86	2.86
4	39.29	21.43	40.71	11.07
5	6.07	3.93	2.14	.71
6	49.29	43.21	22.50	11.43

- The concept of productive vs. non-productive anxiety was also meaningful, as productive anxiety was an inevitable accompaniment to the life changes subjects made as a result of their treatment experience with EFP, but required that women stay present and not dissociate.

- At the post treatment measure 3 of the six women had a "spike" in dissociative symptoms, in spite of an otherwise steady downward trend. Could this have been a response to end-of-treatment anxiety often experienced at the end of a successful group treatment?

Outcome Questionnaire™ – OQ – 45
Assesses 'treatment effectiveness overall'

- Designed to quantify overall treatment effectiveness measuring
    — Symptom distress
    — Interpersonal functioning
    — Role satisfaction
- **Scores over 63 indicate clinical concern**
- Mean scores dropped substantially
- Pre treatment mean score: 93.33 (high even for an outpatient sample)
- Post treatment mean score: 64.33
- Follow up mean score: 58.16

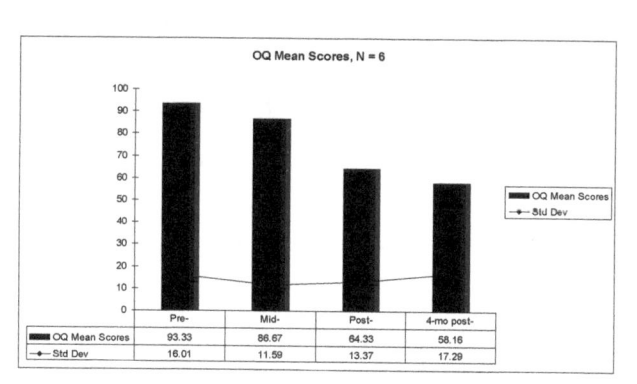

OQ Mean Scores, N = 6

	Pre-	Mid-	Post-	4-mo post-
OQ Mean Scores	93.33	86.67	64.33	58.16
Std Dev	16.01	11.59	13.37	17.29

- By follow up the mean score was within the parameters of a non-clinical sample
- Statistically significant change for both pre to post (p=0.0017) and pre to follow-up (p=0.011)

Outline of Group Sessions
Screening appointment, treatment contract and all release forms completed in advance of group

- WEEK 1
    — Data Collection
    — Opening Exercise, intros, group agreements
    — 20 min on effects of trauma on brain: neural pathways, heightened awareness, autonomic arousal
    — Authentic self and false self
    — Horse observation and intros, safety demo, discussion
- WEEK 2
    — Group process check in
    — Meeting: How the Brain Acts out Trauma: limbic templates
    — Emotional message chart
    — Somatic awareness/body scan
    — Meet the herd, exploring resonance, horse choosing
- WEEK 3
    — Group process time
    — Meeting on meds, empowerment in regards to med choices
    — Handout: Dynamics of shared emotion
    — Just being: reflective sessions w/ horses
- WEEK 4
    — Group process time
    — Meeting Boundaries
    — Somatic skill: learning to manage arousal level
    — Reflective sessions – cont.
- WEEK 5
    — Group process time
    — The language of feeling, tone and touch
    — Grooming, qualities of touch, having horse stand still (ground tie)

Outline of Group Sessions – Continued

- WEEK 6
  - —Data Collection
  - —Group process time
  - —Sensory-motor integration handout
  - —Yielding exercises, leading, turns
- WEEK 7
  - —Group process time
  - —Moving horse in round pen
  - —Initiating play, modulating arousal
  - —Active round pen work and join up
- WEEK 8
  - —Group process time
  - —Finish active round pen sessions
- WEEK 9
  - —Group process time
  - —Skills for authentic relationships & communities
  - —Meeting: trauma as initiation, the wounded healer, the work of developing the gift
  - —Practice for graduation exercise, obstacle course, a walk through the pasture
- WEEK 10
  - —Data collection
  - —Group process time
  - —Graduation activity – a walk through the woods (Horse dance as an alternate for rain)
- 4 MONTHS POST-TREATMENT
  - —Data collection
  - —Social meeting

11.

Therapeutic Considerations for Working with Trauma Survivors in EFP

- It is essential that the therapist present be experienced at containing extreme dissociative states if they occur
- The therapist should be familiar with all the diagnostic categories which have a co-occurrence with trauma as well as being knowledgeable about current methods and theories for treating trauma
- You must keep the groups small
- The group process and the horse activities must be carefully managed in order to create emotional safety
- Attentiveness to, gentle maintenance of, and absolute clarity about boundaries is one of the main structures upon which trust is built
- Many trauma survivors are ultra-sensitive and in their work with the horses you will see their keen intuition validated often

12.

Research at HEAL 2008

A replication of the 2006 pilot study (Shambo et al., 2010) was done in 2008 at HEAL. Measures remained the same, with the exception that the Hamilton Depression Scale was replaced with the Beck Depression Inventory; and we collected qualitative data, using a semi-structured written interview. A thorough discussion of both the quantitative and qualitative data can be found in Zasloff (2009). There were a total of 10 female participants in 2008.[*] The data from Zasloff's thesis is summarized in Slides 13-22.

For more information contact the author of this unpublished Master's Thesis accepted by Lewis and Clark College, Portland, OR. Randy H. Zasloff, MS 503-705-5928 flowshepard@gmail.com

---

Equine Facilitated Psychotherapy

An Outcome Study

Masters Thesis
Randy H Zasloff
May 2009

13.

Acknowledgements: The author extends thanks to Cascade Mental Health Care, in Chehalis WA, and to Human-Equine Alliances for Learning for their support of this ongoing study of EFPL.

---

[*] Informed consent to participate in the study was obtained from all participants (and guardian of youth participants). Study design and implementation approved by Lewis and Clark College Human Subjects Research Committee in 2008; the same design was implemented with oversight from HEAL Board of Directors in 2009, 2010 and 2011.

Unique Qualities Horses Bring to Therapy

- Mirror & provide self-object experiences
- Build attachment with a safe partner
- Relationship in the here and now
- Ability to find & show incongruity
- Provide a connection to the natural world
- Act a metaphor for client issues
- Nonverbal experience

14.

EFP Uniquely Suited for Trauma

- From an Interpersonal Neurobiology perspective:

   "...integrating modalities from the left and right hemispheres enable traumatic memories to be processed in a new manner that allows resolution to occur."

   Siegel (2003)

15.

Method

- Modeled on pilot study (2006) - women with 'complex' PTSD
- Brief treatment - 10 weeks
- EFP in conjunction with psycho-education & cognitive behavioral therapy
- Measures: BDI, BAI, DES, OQ-45
- Pre-, mid-, post, and follow up measurement points
- Qualitative questions; post & follow up

16.

Participants

- 10 adult women with complex PTSD/& or Borderline Personality Disorder & other (depression, substance abuse, anorexia...)
- Referred by local county mental health clinic or if they expressed an interest in EFPL
- Currently in therapy for 2 years or more with no reduction or resolution of symptoms
- No severe allergies to horses/asthma
- Walk on uneven ground & lift, push, or pull 20# or more

17.

Results Summary

- Hypothesis 1: Significant reduction in depression
- Hypothesis 2: Reduced anxiety
- Hypothesis 3: Dissociation
- Hypothesis 4: OQ - clinically improved
- Hypothesis 5: Confirmed: Clients report horses are a positive & important element in healing
- Hypothesis 6: Confirmed: EFPL positively impacted lives & clients are using skills

18.

Discussion

- Intractable depression a feature of trauma (Herman): consistent with EFP outcome study results
- Meinersmann, Bradberry, & Roberts (2008) interviewed women survivors of abuse about their experience of EFP and identified four patterns that reflect the findings of the qualitative portion of this outcome study

19.

Discussion

Patterns	Outcome Themes
I Can Have Power	Empowerment, confidence, boundaries
Doing It Hands On	Confidence, somatic awareness, self-awareness
Horse as Co-Therapist	Trust, love, bonding, mirror, self-esteem
Turned My Life Around	Confidence, self-efficacy, feeling better

Discussion

- Therapeutic Relationship
    - Themes from qualitative data regarding relationship between client & horse mirror the relationship between client and human therapist
    - Attachment theory, intersubjectivity, & interpersonal neurobiology apply to the client/horse relationship
    - York, Adams, and Coady (2008) examined the therapeutic value of equine-human bonding in recovery from trauma and found that the relationship, "suggests parallels between good equine-human relationships and good therapist-client relationships, both, in terms of the bonds that are formed and their healing qualities." (p. 25)

Discussion: Significance

- Adds to the literature supporting EFP as an effective modality
- Supports previous research & shows EFP can be beneficial for adults with PTSD & co-occurring disorders including: BPD, MDD, OCD, Substance Abuse & Dependence, & Eating Disorders

APPENDIX B

Practitioner Pathways for EFPL

I frequently serve as mentor and coach for students new to the field of EFPL as well as experienced practitioners implementing EFPL within their practice setting. Aspiring practitioners have choices that shape and inform the social-emotional skill set needed for EFPL. Make a commitment to becoming the most skilled human service professional you can be, in your chosen field of psychotherapy, counseling or education. This is especially important if you wish to work with vulnerable or at-risk populations.

The lead professional for an EFPL team, responsible for program and treatment planning, should have appropriate legal and ethical credentials for working with the clients to be served. For standards in this area we can look to the Certification Board for Equine Interaction Professionals. CBEIP is the only *independent* certification available for EFPL practitioners. The requirements for CBEIP Certification are based on education, experience in EFPL and an impartial, skills-based examination. This board stipulates that candidates have a minimum of Masters degree or equivalent education in a field of psychology, social work, counseling or education. The CBEIP website is http://www.cbeip.org/ .

Other members of the EFPL team should access suitable training in EFPL skill sets, including horsemanship advancement and academic classes to help them understand areas like human development, empathic responding, or basic psychology. Training programs in EFPL, including the HEAL Facilitator Training Program, offer training in a specific model, and award a "certificate of completion." This certifies that the candidate met and completed the requirements of a particular program. Standards for these programs may vary considerably.

A cautionary note to beginning practitioners—do not use the word "therapy" or "psychotherapy" to describe your EFPL services, unless you are legally qualified to practice as a therapist in your state or province. In the US the license to practice mental health counseling or therapy is administered by each states' board of public health.

Some of the major organizations that offer training in EFPL are listed below. The list is not inclusive and should not be considered an endorsement but will provide good starting points for an internet search.

Adventures in Awareness – http://www.adventuresinawareness.net/

Equine Assisted Growth and Learning Association (EAGALA) – http://www.eagala.org/

Epona Equestrian Services – http://www.eponaquest.com/

Federation of Horses in Education and Therapy International AISBL (HETI) – http://www.frdi.net/

Human-Equine Alliances for Learning (HEAL) – http://www.humanequinealliance.org/

PATH International (PATH, Intl) – http://www.pathintl.org/

REFERENCES

Bizub, A. L., Joy, A. and Davidson, L. (2003). "It's Like Being in Another World": Demonstrating the benefits of therapeutic horseback riding for individuals with psychiatric disability. *Psychiatric Rehabilitation Journal, 26*(4), 377-84.

Blakeslee, Sandra and Blakeslee, Matthew. (2007). *The Body Has a Mind of its Own.* New York: Random House.

Burgon, H. (2003). Case studies of adults receiving horse-riding therapy. *Anthrozoos, 16*(3), 263-276.

Doidge, Norman. (2007). *The Brain That Changes Itself.* New York: Penguin Books.

EAGALA (Equine Assisted Growth and Learning Association). http://www.eagala.org/

Epona Equestrian Services. http://eponaquest.com/

Federation of Horses in Education and Therapy International AISBL (originally the *Federation of Riding for the Disabled International*). http://www.frdi.net/about.html

Fine, A. (Ed.). (2000). *Handbook on Animal-Assisted Therapy.* San Diego, CA: Academic Press.

Firestone, Robert, Firestone, Lisa, and Catlett, Joyce. (2002). *Conquer Your Critical Inner Voices.* Oakland, CA: New Harbinger Publications.

Fruzzetti, Alan E. Ph.D., (2006). *The High Conflict Couple, a Dialectical Behavior Therapy Guide to Finding Peace, Intimacy & Validation.* Oakland, CA: New Harbinger Publications. Inc.

Goleman, Daniel. (1996). *Emotional Intelligence: Why it can matter more than IQ.* New York: Bantam Dell.

Grandin, Temple. (1995). *Thinking in Pictures: My Life with Autism.* New York: Random House.

Grandin, Temple and Johnson, Catherine. (2005). *Animals in Translation.* Orlando, FL: Harcourt Books.

Grandin, Temple and Johnson, Catherine. (2009). *Animals Make Us Human.* Orlando, FL: Houghton-Mifflin Harcourt.

Hart, L. (2000). Methods, Standards, Guidelines and Considerations in Selecting Animals for Animal-Assisted Therapy. In A. Fine (Ed.), *Handbook on Animal-Assisted Therapy* (pp. 93-94). San Diego, CA: Academic Press.

Hempfling, Klaus Ferdinand. (2004). *What Horses Reveal.* North Pomfret, VT: Trafalger Square Publishing.

Hempfling, Klaus Ferdinand. *Coming Together.* [DVD] North Pomfret, VT: Trafalgar Square Books. http://www.horseandriderbooks.com/

Herman, J. (1997). *Trauma and Recovery.* New York: Basic Books.

Ingram, Kathleen Barry. http://www.sacredplaceofpossibility.com/

Institute of HeartMath. http://www.heartmath.org/

Jackson, Jaime. (2010). *Paddock Paradise: A Natural Guide to Horse Boarding*. Fayatteville, AR: Star Ridge Publishing.

Killilay, Sue, Director of Cascade Mental Health Care, Chehalis, WA. Personal communication, April 19, 2010

Kohanov, L. (2001). *The Tao of Equus*, Novato, CA: New World Library.

Kohanov, Linda. (2003). *Riding Between the Worlds*. Novato, CA: New World Library.

Kohanov, Linda. (November, 2007). Epona Approved Instructor Reunion Meeting.

Kohanov, Linda. Also see Epona Equestrian Services. http://eponaquest.com/

Lavender, Don. (2006). *Equine-Utilised Psychotherapy*. London: Mrunalini Press Limited.

Lewis, Thomas, Amini, Fari and Lannon, Richard. (2000). *A General Theory of Love*. New York: Random House, Inc.

Linehan, M. (1993). *Cognitive-Behavioral Treatment of Borderline Personality Disorder* (pp 51-56). New York: The Guilford Press.

McCormick, A. & McCormick, M. (1997). *Horse Sense and the Human Heart*. Deerfield Park, FL: Health Communications Inc.

McLean, L.M. (2004). Childhood Sexual Abuse and Adult Psychiatric Diagnosis: Current Views and Clinical Implications. *Current Medical Literature: Psychiatry, 15*(2):29-34.

Mistral, Kip. (2005). Heart to Heart: A Quantitative Approach to Measuring the Emotional Bond between Horses and Humans, *Horse Connection Magazine* August 2007. Available at: http://www.horseconnection.com/site/archive/story-aug07.html

Moreau, Leslie and McDaniel, Boo. (2001). *Equine Facilitated Mental Health: A Field Guide for Practice*. Available through Boo McDaniel, 13 Pony Farm Lane, Temple, NH 03084 USA. http://www.ponyfarm.com/

Murdock, Karen, and Lukas. http://www.playingwithlukas.com/

Ogden, Pat, Minton, Kekuni and Pain, Clare. (2006). *Trauma and the Body: A Sensorimotor Approach to Psychotherapy*. New York: Norton and Company.

Panksepp, Jaak. (1998). *Affective Neuroscience: The Foundations of Human and Animal Emotions*. New York: Oxford University Press.

Pankseepp, Jaak. (2011). Decoding Primal Affective Experiences of Humans and Related Animals, *PLoS ONE, 3* August 2011, Volume 6, Issue 8. http://www.plosone.org/

PATH International (Professional Association for Therapeutic Horsemanship International). http://www.pathintl.org/resources-education/workshops/equine-specialist

Perry, Bruce and Hambrick, Erin. (2008). The Neurosequential Model of Therapeutics. *Reclaiming Children and Youth, Volume 17*, No 3. http://www.childtrauma.org/index.php/articles/cta-neurosequential-model

Pignon, Frederick and Delgado, Magali. (2009). *Gallop to Freedom*. North Pomeroy, VT: Trafalger Square Books.

Porges, Stephen. (2011). *The Polyvagal Theory: Neurophysiological Foundations of Emotions, Attachment, Communication and Self-Regulation*. New York: Norton and Company.

Pryor, Karen. (2002). *Don't Shoot the Dog: The New Art of Teaching and Training*. Great Britain: Cox and Wyman Ltd.

Rashid, Mark. (2000). *Horses Never Lie: The Heart of Passive Leadership*. Boulder, CO: Johnson Books.

Rector, Barbara K. (2005). *Adventures in Awareness: Learning with the Help of Horses*. Bloomington, IN: AuthorHouse. Also see: http://adventuresinawareness.net/

Reiner, Robert. (2008). Integrating a Portable Biofeedback Device into Clinical Practice for Patients Who Have Anxiety Disorders. *Applied Psychophysiological Biofeedback*, 33:55 61 February 2008, pp. 59-61.

Reivich, Karen Ph.D., and Schatte, Andrew Ph.D. (2002). *The Resilience Factor*. New York: Broadway Books.

Rivas, Mim Eichler. (2005). *Beautiful Jim Key: The Lost History of a Horse and a Man Who Changed the World*. New York: William Morrow (An imprint of HarperCollins).

Rogers, Annie G. (1996). *A Shining Affliction: A Story of Healing and Harm in Psychotherapy*. New York: Penguin Books.

Roth, S., Newman, E., Pelcovitz, D., van der Kolk, B., & Mandel, F. (1997). Complex PTSD in Victims Exposed to Sexual and Physical Abuse: Results from the DSM-IV Field Trial for Post-traumatic Stress Disorder. *Journal of Traumatic Stress, 10*(4), 539-55.

Rothschild, Babette. (2000). *The Body Remembers: The Psychophysiology of Trauma and Trauma Treatment*. New York: Norton and Company.

Schultz, P. N., Remick-Barlow, G. and Robbins, L. (2007). Equine-assisted psychotherapy: a mental health promotion/intervention modality for children who have experienced intra-family violence. *Health & Social Care in the Community, 15*(3):265-71.

Shambo L., Seely S. K., and Vonderfecht, H. (2010). A Pilot Study on Equine-Facilitated Psychotherapy for Trauma-Related Disorders, *Scientific and Educational Journal of Therapeutic Riding 2010* ISSN 1174-6238.

Siegel, Daniel J. MD, (1999). *The Developing Mind: How Relationships and the Brain Interact to Shape Who We Are*. New York: Guilford, Inc.

Siegel, Daniel. (2010). *Mindsight: The New Science of Personal Transformation*. New York: Random House, Inc.

Stress Eraser. http://www.stresseraser.com/

Szalavitz, Maia and Perry, Bruce. (2010). *Born for Love: Why Empathy is Essential—and Endangered.* New York: Harper Collins Publishers.

Trotter, K. S. (2006, March). The Effectiveness of Equine Assisted Group Counseling with At Risk Children and Adolescents. Paper presented at the American Counseling Association International Conference, Pittsburgh, PA. http://www.unt.edu/etd/all/Dec2006/Open/trotter_kay_sudekum/index.htm

Tyler, J. T. (1994). Equine psychotherapy: Worth more than just a horse laugh. *Women & Therapy, 15*(3/4), 139-47.

van der Hart, O., Nijenhuis, E. R. & Steele, K. (2005). Dissociation: An insufficiently recognized major feature of *complex* posttraumatic stress disorder. *Journal of Traumatic Stress, 18*(5), 413-23.

Van der Kolk, B. & Courtois, Christine A. (2005). Editorial Comments: Complex Developmental Trauma. *Journal of Traumatic Stress, 18*(5), 385-388.

Webb, W., & Pearlman, C. (2002). *It's Not About the Horse: It's About Overcoming Fear and Self-Doubt.* Carlsbad, CA: Hay House, Inc.

Young, David. See website: http://www.HRVresearch.com/

Zasloff, Randy. (2009). Equine-Facilitated Psychotherapy: An Outcome Study. Unpublished Masters' Thesis accepted by Lewis & Clark College School of Education and Counseling. Available from author at http://www.findingflowcounseling.com/

INDEX

10 point arousal scale, *34*

A General Theory of Love, 17, 21, 25, 99
abandonment, 43, 48, 54, 79, 99, 104, 106
abstraction, 21, 111
active work (with horses), 66
Adventures in Awareness, 33, 131
Affective Neuroscience, 20, 39, 65, 91, 93
amygdala hijack, 19
anchor, 11, 36, 92, 95
Animal Assisted Therapy (AAT), 117
Animals Make Us Human, 25
anxiety, 3, 12, *24*, 27, 30, 36, 54–57, 61–64, 86, 93, 97, 103, 104, 105, *121, 122, 123, 129*
approaches (to EFPL), 8–9, 12–13, 44, 95
archetype, 23, 83, 87, 88
arousal, 11, *18*, 21–23, 27, 29–35, 38, 39, 42–46, 48, 49, 54, 55, 56, 57, 58, 59, 60, 61, 62, 63, 64, 70–72, 78, 97, 99, 110
A Shining Affliction, 22
assessment, 3, 4, 10, 27, 53, 80, 111, 114
attachment, 3, 8, 11, 14, 18, 19, 21, 24, 55, 92–95, 99, 111, *128*
Autonomic Nervous System (ANS), 13, 17–20, *18, 20*, 22, 29, 32, 37, 42, 55, 62–63
avoidance, 30, 54, 62, 111

Beau, 26, 49, 73, 86, 100
Beck Depression Inventory, 127
Behavioral Assessment System for Children (BASC), 118
Blakeslee, Sandra and Blakeslee, Matthew, 41, 50–51
body awareness, *24*, 58
Body-Centered Awareness, 29, 31
body image, 51, 80
body language, 1, 12, 32, 41, 47, 48, 67
body scan, 57–59, 61, 104, *124*
bonding, 19, 20–22, 24, 26, 28, 91, 92, 95, 117, *130*
Borderline Personality Disorder, 1, 119, *129*
bottom-up, 36, *39*, 39, 53, *75*, 111
boundaries, 10, 13–14, *24,* 25–27, 41–48, 50, 51, 56, 58, 60, 61, 62, 63, 68, 83, 86, 92, 97, 98, 99, 100, 104, 105, 110, *125, 130*
brainstem, 11, 17–21, 30, 33, 53, 60, 62, 71, 82, 84, 99
breathing, 14, 15, 19, 29, 30–33, 35, 36, 37, 38, 57, 70, 80–82, 96
bridging cue, 84

Burgon, H., 118

CARE circuit, *24*, 24, 92, *93*, 99, 100
Cascade Mental Health Care, xiii, xv, 28, 111, 127
cause-and-effect thinking, 21
challenge approach, 9
challenge exercises, 69
charging the clicker, 84
children, x, 3, 8, 15, 33, 88, 94, 107, 113, 117
Children's Global Assessment Functioning, 117
clicker training, 84, *85*, 85
Cloud, 61, 86, 98, 100
cognition, 72
cognitive, 9, 32, *34*, 35, 37, 38, *39*, 55, 62, 64, 84, 111, 113–114, *128*
communication, 14, *24*, 43, 48, 63, 65, 67–68, 71, 74, 79, 96, 111
congruence, 44, 48, 85, 98
Conquer Your Critical Inner Voices, 53
cortex, 11, 17, *18*, 36, 62, 64, 70, 84
counseling, 111, 118, *121*, 131

DeKunffy, Charles, 67
denial, 89
diagnosis, 10, 27, 118
diagnostic categories, 21, 118, *125*
dissociation, *18*, 47, 54, 62, 63, 104, 118, *121, 123*
dissociative, 119, *123*
Divided Self, *24*, 53, 55
Dixsi, 72, *85*, 98
Doidge, Norman, 21, 22, 77–78
drawing position (in horsemanship), 67, *76*
driving position (in horsemanship), 69, *76*
dysfunction, 3, *18*, 27, 42
dysregulated, 21, 62, 63

EFPL debriefing, 10–11, 96
emotion, ix, xi, 3, 4, 11, 12, 14, 17, 21, 25, 28, 39, 54, 55, 58, 62, 63, 72, 78, 80, 87, 89, 98, 109, *124*
emotional age, 8
emotional contagion, 14
Emotional Intelligence, 62
emotional regulation, 11, 23–24, 59
emotional resonance, 14, 24, 49, 59
emotional response, 13, 21
emotional restructuring, 13
emotional ruminations, 21

emotional safety, 1, 7, 8, 114, *125*
empathy, 21, 24, 85, 94
energy awareness, 9
energy field, 46
enmeshment, 58
Epona Equestrian Services, xiii, 9, 132
equestrian liability policy, 11, 12
Equine Assisted Growth and Learning Association (EAGALA), xiii, 9, 131
Equine-Facilitated Mental Health, 8
Equine-Facilitated Psychotherapy and Learning (EFPL), ix, xiii, 1–4, *definition* 7
Equine-Facilitated Psychotherapy for Trauma-Related Disorders, 117, *120*
experiential process work, 111
experiential psychotherapy, 7
extinction, 79, 85

facilitate, 4, 41, 66, 110, 111
facilitator, xiii, 4, 85, *120*, 131
false self, 61, 81, 87, *124*
family dynamics, 84
FEAR neural circuit, 25, 30, 42, 62, 99
Federation of Horses in Education and Therapy International (AISBL), 132
fight or flight 19, 22, 53, 54, 87
Fine, A., 117
Firestone, Robert, Firestone, Lisa, and Catlett, Joyce, 53
Frieda, xii, 15, 38, *47*, 87, 88, 105, 106
Fruzzetti, Alan E. Ph.D., 62

Galant, 5, *47*, 95, 106
Gem, 15, 26, 87, 88
Gestalt psychotherapy, 111
Goleman, Daniel, 62
Grandin, Temple, 22, 23, 25, 66, 78, 80, 97, 99, 111
grooming, 81, 95, *124*
grounding, 30, 44, 55, 80, 94
group process, 100, 119, *125*
groups, x, 3, 8, 9, 12, 24, 25, 28, 36, 44, 111, 117, 118, *125*

hang out zone, 45, 47
Hart, L., 1, 117
Heart Rate Variability (HRV), 37
Hempfling, Klaus Ferdinand, 88
herd observation, 94
Herman, J., 118, 119, *129*
home run, 11, 78
horse dancing, 81, 82
horse decoration, 81
horsemanship, ix, xi, 13, 14, 22, 23, 66, 68, 69, 71, 76, 84, 85, 86, 98, 104, 131
horse specialist, 2, 9, 11, 12, 14, 68, 97
Human-Equine Alliances for Learning (HEAL), ix, xiii, xiv, xv, xvi, 1–4, 7–15, 23–25, 27, 28, 31, 34, 37, 38, 45, 50, 54, 61, 66, 69, 71, 72, 76, 81, 82, 84, 85, 86, 87, 92, 95, 97, 98, 100, 104, 105, 106, 110, 111, 113, 114, 117, *120*, 127, 131, 132
hypervigilance, *34*, *121*

imagination, *24*, 72, 77, 78, 79, 80, 82, 86, 87–89
incongruence, 12, 48, 55, 117
Ingram, Kathleen Barry, xiii, 57, 58, 113
instincts, ix, 13, 19, 71
instruction, 32, 37, 56, 59, 82
internal states, 58
intimacy, 13, 42, 43, 58, 91, 94, 103
intuition, 29, 37, 66, 81, 89, *125*

Jilly, 97–98
join-up, 14, 15, 68–71, *76*, 76, 80, 85

Key Five, *24*, 78, 80–81, 83, 86, 89
Key Four, *24*, 65, 67–68, 72, 73
Key One, *24*, 29, 32–37, 38
Key Six, *24*, 91, 94, 99, 100
Key Three, *24*, 54, 55
Key Two, *24*, 41, 44, 49, 50
Killilay, Sue, 111
Kohanov, Linda, xiii, 9, 44, 117–119

Lavender, Don, 4, 13, 43, 55, 109
leadership, 13, 66, 68–69, 105
Lewis, Thomas, Amini, Fari, and Lannon, Richard, xiii, 17, 21, 22, 23, 25, 53, 93, 99, 127
life experience, 8, 55
limbic care, 13
limbic connection, 13–14, 23, 60, 66, 68, 79, 80, 84, 94, 96, 101
Limbic Questions for EFPL Facilitation, 60
limbic revision, 14, 21, 25
limbic system, 3, 11, 17, 20–22, 60, 62, 70, 71
Linehan, M., 63, 119
LUST neural circuit, 92

mammalian brain, 17, *18*, *20*, 20, 48, 91–92, 95
mandalas, 50
McCormick, A. and McCormick, D., xiii, 117
meet and greet, 43, 44, *47*, 47
Meeting the Herd, 32, 36
mindfulness, 4, 15, 29, 31, 35, 37, 38, 58, 94
Mindsight, 29
mirroring, 45, *76*
music, 33, 81–82, 100, 106

navigate by feeling, 110
negative reinforcement, 84
neocortex, *18*, 19
nervous system, *18*, 19, *20*, 22, 30, 74, 87, 110
neural pathways, 11, 13, *18*, 21, 22, 25, 29, 30, 32, 43, 54, 55, 81, 114, *124*

neurobiological, 8
neuroplasticity, 21, 77
neuroscience, 2, 4, 17, 54, 117
North American Riding for the Handicapped Association (NARHA), xiv, 2, 8, 119

operant conditioning, 84
opioid, 92
oxytocin, *24*, 24, 92, 99

PANIC neural circuit, *24*, 25, 42, 54, 62, 95, 99
Panksepp, Jaak, 17, 20, 22, 23, *24*, 24, 25, 30, 39, 42, 65, 78, 79, 91, 92, 93, 95, 99
PATH International, xiii, 2, 7–8, 132
peripersonal space, 50
Perry, Bruce, 18, 22
personal growth, 100
PLAY neural circuit, 25, 66, 72, 80
Porges, Stephen, 42
positive choices, 9
positive reinforcement, 84
Post-Traumatic Stress Disorder (PTSD), 1–4, 8, 21, 25, 27, 28, 30, 49, 62, 73, 86, 100, 103–105, 107, 111, 114, 118, 119, *121*, *123*, *128–130*
procedures, 57, 59, 70
projection, 37, 89, 100, 110
psychoeducational, 10
psychology, x, xi, xiv, 2, 4, 9, 107, 117, 131
psychosocial, 8, 11

qualitative data, 25, 127, *130*

RAGE neural circuit, 23, *24*, 25, 42, 54, 62, 99
Rector, Barbara K, 23, 33
reflective sessions, 55, 56, 58, *124*
regulation, 11, 14, 21, 22, 23, 24, 30, 33, 38, *39*, 54, 57, 59, 67, 69, 71, 82, 93, 96, 97, 118, 119
Reivich, Karen Ph.D., and Schatte, Andrew Ph.D., 62, 63
Remuda Ranch, 103–105
research, xv, 1, 2, 3, 37, 66, 72, 111, 114, 119, *130*
resonance, 14, 21, 24, 25, 49, 57, 59, 61, 71, 83, 88, *124*
respect, 23, *24*, 26, 42, 43, 44, 48, 71, 72, 82, 105
responsibility, 23, 41, 43, 88, 94, 97, 98, 113
riding, ix, xi, xii, xiii, 3, 7, 8, 10, 14, 45, 68, 69, 98, 104, 110, 118
Rogers, Annie G., 22
Roth, S., Newman, E., Pelcovitz, D., van der Kolk, B., and Mandel, F., 118
Rothschild, Babette, 18, 31
round pen, xii, xiii, 10, 14, 59, 68, 69, 70, 71, 72, 73, 80, 81, 82, 84, 100, *125*
rumination, *39*, 63

safety, x, 1, 7, 8, 12, 14, 18, 22, 23, 24, 28, 30, 31, 32, 33, 36, 42, 43, 49, 56, 57, 59, 60, 65, 66, 67, 72, 74, 79, 80, 82, 87, 97, 111, 114, 117, *124*, *125*

schema, 50, 51
SEEKING neural circuit, 4, *24*, 25, 42, 78, 79–80, 84, 87, 89, 99, 109
self-regulate, 21, 27, 70, 117
self-soothing habits, 11, 55, 97
shamanic experiences, 9
Shambo, Leigh, 2, 25, 72, 117, *120*, 127
Siegel, Daniel, 21–22, 29, 57, 62–63, *128*
social-emotional learning, 17
soft eyes (in horsemanship), 46
somatic, 27, 29, 30, 31, 44, 50, 55, 56, 63, 89, 111, 119, *121*, *130*
spatial relationship, 43
stereotypy, 97
stress management, 97
structure, 7, 8, 14, 17, 22, 36, 45, 57, 67, 69, 70, 82, 92, 94, 95, 96
Sympathetic Nervous System, *20*, 62

Taoism, 65
The Body Remembers, 31
therapeutic riding, xv
therapeutic strategy, 10
Thinking in Pictures, 80
top-down, *39*, 39, *75*
trauma, 9, 10, 18, 29, *34*, 117, *120*, *124*, *125*, *128*
treatment goals, 3, 7, 8, 9, 10, 11, 80
treatment plan, 10, 11
treatment setting, 1, 3, 114
triggers, 8, *24*, 53, 61, 62, 87
triune brain, 17, *18*, 18, 53
trust, xii, 13, *24*, 26, 30, 42, 43, 49, 67, 68, 69, 71, 72, 78, 79, 81, 92, 94, 95, 98, 101, 104, 110, 113, 114, *125*
type of client, 7, 9, 32
type of program, 7

unresolved history, 10, 12, 29, 47, 57, 60, 96, 97

valence, 35, 46
violence, 3, 9, 18, 117, 118, 135
vulnerability, 55, 56, 57, 58, 63, 79, 80, 86, 100, 105, 109, 110, 114

What Horses Reveal, 88
Williamson, Marianne, 107
window of tolerance, 11, 44, 49, 54, 55, 57, 62, 63, 70, 91, 99

Yin and Yang, *24*, 65, 67, 69, 73, *75*
Young, David, xv, 2, 9, 37, *85*, 89, 109
youth, ix, 3, 9, 25, 44, 46, 69, 84, 127

Zasloff, Randy, xv, 25, 127